State Management

An enquiry into models of public administration and management

Jan-Erik Lane

Routledge
Taylor & Francis Group

LONDON AND NEW YORK

For Dean Beat Bürgenmeier – a great admirer
of Max Weber in the University of Geneva

First published 2009
by Routledge
2 Park Square, Milton Park, Abingdon, Oxon OX14 4RN

Simultaneously published in the USA and Canada
by Routledge
270 Madison Avenue, New York, NY 10016

Routledge is an imprint of the Taylor & Francis Group, an informa business

© 2009 Jan-Erik Lane

Typeset in Times New Roman by Swales & Willis Ltd, Exeter, Devon
Printed and bound in Great Britain by Antony Rowe, Chippenham, Wiltshire

British Library Cataloguing in Publication Data
A catalogue record for this book is available from the British Library

Library of Congress Cataloging in Publication Data
A catalog record for this book has been requested

ISBN10: 0–415–49234–3 (hbk)
ISBN10: 0–415–49235–1 (pbk)
ISBN10: 0–203–87988–0 (ebk)

ISBN13: 978–0–415–49234–8 (hbk)
ISBN13: 978–0–415–49235–5 (pbk)
ISBN13: 978–0–203–87988–7 (ebk)

State Management

State Management offers a comprehensive yet concise introduction to the new field of state management, presenting an analysis of basic questions within the theories of bureaucracy, policy-making, principal–agent modelling and policy networks. Focussing upon recent state transformation, it illuminates public sector reform strategies such as New Public Management as well as incorporation, tendering and bidding, decentralisation, team production and privatisation.

This book argues that we should look upon the variety of models or approaches to public management or public administration as all belonging under *state management*. The so-called "working state" in a well-ordered society involves government delivering services, paying for social security and respecting the rule of law. In this text, Jan-Erik Lane systematically examines the key approaches to the study of how government attempts to achieve these goals, discussing the pros and cons of alternative frameworks of analysis and exploring the relevance of the principal–agent approach.

Each chapter discusses a different issue within state management that is integral to the broader debate, including:

- Public regulation
- The relationship between the law and the state
- Combining ecology and policy-making
- Multi-level governance
- The virtues and vices of public–private partnerships
- Policy implementation.

Presenting a clear overview of how the state operates when government sets out to deliver public services, and generating questions to encourage new research, *State Management* is a valuable new text for both undergraduate and postgraduate courses in political science, public administration and public management.

Jan-Erik Lane has taught as a professor in several universities around the globe. He has published numerous books and articles on many topics in political science. He was professor at the University of Geneva between 1996 and 2008 and is now Mercator visiting professor at the University of Heidelberg.

Contents

Preface

While management is the academic discipline that models how private firms operate, public management or public administration targets the public sector in an encompassing fashion, covering government at all levels, independent regulatory boards as well as public enterprises. This book suggests that we look upon the variety of models or approaches to public management or public administration as all belonging under *state management*. A key issue in state management is whether private management is entirely different from public management, given the distinction between the market and the state, the public and the private or economics and politics.

How do governments get the job done in providing services to their populations? This is the core question in theories of state management, i.e. organisation of the delivery of services in the public sector. It has received many different answers that will be surveyed in this book, subsuming them under a parsimonious set of models. The purpose is to identify the different models of the so-called output side of government, i.e. how the units that deliver public services operate.

Since the emergence of New Public Management (NPM) in the 1980s, there has been a tension between NPM and traditional public administration as academic disciplines, meaning that we perceive a split between two sets of approaches to be employed when organising the public sector. The time has come to bridge this gap by showing that state management hosts a diversity of models with which one may analyse government outputs and outcomes.

This book surveys the main theories of state management, enquiring into the different modes of organising the state from the perspective of public services delivery. It summarises my teaching of public administration and NPM since the late 1970s, from my teaching at Umea University, Sweden to my courses in China: Chinese University of Hong Kong, Hong Kong University, Fudan University, and in Beijing. Economist Bürgenmeier suggested the title of this book, being an expert on private management. In the Conclusion, I have drawn upon the article "Strategic Management in the Public Sector: More than an Algorithm" published in *The British Journal of Leadership in Public Services* (2008), Volume 2, Issue 3.

Jan-Erik Lane
Heidelberg, March 2009

Introduction

Is public management different from private sector management?

Introduction

Management is a major field of study in economics and the social sciences. It forms an integral part of business administration as well as in organisational analysis. During the post-Second World War period thousands of articles and books have been published in this area under the labels of "Strategy", "Organisational Behaviour" or "Culture and Leadership in Organisation". Given such an effort to understand how private firms operate, their goals, structures and results, one cannot avoid the question of the relevance of management for the analysis of the public sector and how government functions.

Management deals with how people are motivated to participate in teams with a definitive structure and leadership in order to produce goods and services. The theories of management were developed in relation to the modern enterprise, often having thousands of employees, working under a specific private law institution, namely, the Limited Liability Company or *aktiengesellschaft*. Given that management modelled the internal operations of large private enterprises, it is not astonishing that it identified formal organisation as a characteristic feature of private sector management. This was a basic similarity with the study of bureaucracy in government. Yet, one must pose in an explicit manner the question of whether public management tends to be more different than similar compared with private management.

In this chapter, I will argue for the *difference thesis*, claiming that politics and the public sector make for several differences between public and private management. Although public management can learn from the many insights in private management, one should not equate them and bypass how different public management tends to be compared with private management.

The state as decisions: policies, laws and money

Economists and political scientists have come to realise that issues of public policy and public finance cannot be solved on the assumption that a government exists only to serve public good or promote public interest. Government must be understood as one of the major institutions of society facing a market for policies (Breton, 2007). The behaviour of government can be cast in a simple demand-supply-equilibrium framework, when one explains the forces that influence and determine the flow of resources as they are allocated between competing ends in the public sector. Demands by citizens stem from maximising their desire for specific public policies and private goods. The supply of public policies by politicians and bureaucrats is determined when they maximise the probability of their re-election and the size of their budgets.

Objectives

Public management is the accomplishment of social objectives, whereas private management is the maximisation of profit for a set of owners. One may express this difference between social objectives and private objectives in various ways, but however it is expressed, it is still valid. Government typically delivers goods and services that are in the common interest of a nation or community. Private enterprises are in the business to make money. Politics enters public management in a decisive manner when the basic goals of the organisations are defined and decided upon.

Insisting upon the separation between governance towards national or community goals on the one hand and profit maximisation on the other does not entail that private enterprises cannot have a multiplicity of objectives and that making money is not an incentive in public management. Of course public enterprises and organisations with user fees are concerned with making money. The huge modern corporation states time and again that it also cares about its employees and the environment besides its profits. On a few occasions, we will have reason to discuss the public choice school which argues that incentives in politics and markets tend to be the same, i.e. the maximisation of selfish motives, including making money. Yet, even if it is true that New Public Management (NPM) underlined the relevance of buying and selling in government operations to an extent not seen before, it remains true that public management has a different goal function from private management.

A number of concepts in political science, sociology and economics have been devised to describe the typical goals of government: the public interest, national interests, collective interests, public goods, externalities, common pool goods, economies of scale, etc. I will employ the term "social objectives" in order to emphasise that public management delivers goods and services to a group that can be as large as a country or even smaller units of the country. The delivery of goods and services for social objectives implies that community considerations that are uniform, tax financed, obligatory, encompassing, etc. play a major role. This is what makes the following list of services public: (1) law and order; (2) infrastructure; (3) education and health care; (4) social security.

One is well reminded of the distinction between provision and production in relation to public services, as it is not necessary to employ a public agency to deliver such services. It can be done through contracting with a private supplier. Actually, this is where models of public management may make a difference as some favour public supply while others allow for contracting out.

Setting

Private management is orientated towards the market, as the market is the final arbiter of a private enterprise. It shapes its destiny in many ways, determining its profitability prospects, at least to a considerable extent. The setting of public management is an entirely different one, comprising politics, power and the chief public institutions of a country. Whether the government is a national, regional or local one, they are the principals of public management, meaning that it is up to them to instruct, fund and monitor public management operations. And they are not "owners" in the same way as shareholders own private corporations, being at the same time the principals of private management.

Whereas individual share owners have full property rights in the corporation in question within the limits of limited liability rules, the members of government have no ownership rights. They manage a trust – the state – in the interests of a group: a nation or a community. Through the political process it is decided what goals this trust should promote. The achievement of these goals may be positive for the members of government, but in itself it gives them no right to share the gains of the community. Individual people delivering public services will demand private compensation for their efforts – the incentive question in public management being extremely important – but they cannot claim ownership.

Many public services are allocated outside of the market, as it is difficult to reveal their value in a correct manner. Thus, public services always come with a cost, but their price is not fully known. The problem of designing ways and methods to reveal consumer preferences for public services has been debated for a long time without arriving at a solution that would be easy to apply. This means that the value of public services tends to reflect the political preferences forthcoming in the democratic election process. The difficulty with the paradoxes in private supply of public services – free rider, preference distortion – is so large that government will employ the political channel to supply these goods and services.

Thus, public management is entrenched in a setting where political bodies – ministries, parliaments, courts – play a major role. The same applies to services provided in the regional or local contexts. The close link between public management and politics shows up in two distinctive features of public management:

1   tax financing
2   public law regulation.

Although user fees are common in public management, taxes constitute the largest income source, especially when obligatory social security charges are classified, as they should be, as taxes. Most taxes are levied without earmarked funding purposes, which is true of income taxes, corporate taxes and inheritance taxes. They are used to cover the costs of providing public services, despite the fact that the value of these services is not revealed simultaneously. Public services are considered valuable when politicians vote appropriations covering their costs of provision.

The provision of public services being handled outside of the market setting, their regulation in terms of access, quality and quantity tends to be regulated by public law instructions. Thus, each and every public service has its legal framework, stating goals, means, funding, etc. This reliance upon general and special administrative law is typical of public management, and accounts for its heavy reliance upon formal organisation and bureaucracy. Private management is basically regulated through private law such as contract law and company law. As a matter of fact, each area of public management – education, fire protection, health care, police, etc. – has its own special administrative law. There is nothing comparable in private law.

Politics against economics

State and market, the public and the private, politics and economics – these classical distinctions in political economy surface when one tries to identify the nature of public management. It used to be the case that public management was handled almost exclusively through bureaucracy or big formal organisations with many employees working under public law schemes. Thus, the authorities, agencies and boards operating under central, regional or local governments constituted public employment, amounting to between 20 and 40 per cent of the workforce. When social security was added to the picture, one arrived at the consolidated public sector which also included social insurance funds. It was pitted against the market sector, comprising the private enterprises and the households with private individuals.

This dichotomous model of society with two completely different sectors operating according to their own logic is not applicable today. There have been so many reforms of the public sector, introducing market mechanisms, that public management is both politics and economics, state and market. Yet, despite all the hollowing out of the public sector during the last twenty years, there is still government and public management, delivering many services. A key question is, of course, how to model public management when it is no longer that monolithic structure of formal organisations called "bureaucracy" (Rabin *et al.*, 1997; Peters and Pierre, 2003).

The major restriction: rule of law

State management cannot be analysed without taking into account the requirements of rule of law. The elements of rule of law that restrain state management are numerous and they constrain public management to an extent that has no correspondence in private management. Thus, to make sure that a state adheres to rule of law, it is vital that the following requirements be met (Lane, 2007):

1 *procedural accountability*: decisions must be taken in accordance with established and known procedures;
2 *legality*: decisions must follow the law of the country that either permits or obliges the state administration to act;
3 *complaint and redress*: in relation to all decisions concerning citizens they must be capable of filing a complaint, expressing their grievances and seeking redress or compensation;
4 *inquiry and responsibility*: the agents providing public services must be capable of being examined and held responsible for their actions or non-actions.

While it is true that private management also faces a set of norms of accountability and responsibility, it is the case that in the public sector, rule of law requirements go further and are more demanding, especially in terms of procedures and documentation.

Public sector reform tends to bypass the implication of rule of law for state management, with the only exception of reforms of human rights. Thus, it has been argued against the NPM philosophy that its emphasis upon efficiency and marketisation squares badly with the requirements for rule of law.

Rule of law is a *sine qua non* in democracies, as it constitutes the basic elements in constitutional democracies besides political participation. Even when a country does not fully adhere to the democratic regime, it often pays respect to some of the rule of law requirements (Lane, 2007).

The problematics of state management

A theory of state management that would be comparable in size and depth to the theory of management in the private sector would have to confront a set of thorny issues that crop up in public organisation and the governance of the public sector:

1   How relevant is the use of the bureaucracy model? The reply to this question depends upon how one evaluates the model, positively or negatively, and for which context it is to be employed.
2   How rational is public policy-making? The answer to this problem depends upon the meaning of rationality in the social sciences as well as upon whether one targets individual behaviour or group behaviour.
3   Is successful implementation possible, and if so *how*? Different replies to the implementation gap have been rendered, but there is, as yet, no conclusive answer about how to achieve implementation.
4   Can the implementation deficit be bridged? Once this riddle in public sector management was uncovered, many replies deserve discussion: agencies, networks or public–private partnerships, internal markets, public joint-stock companies.
5   Can one say something about the most profound problems in public management? Weber suggested the risk of appropriation of the public resources, but more recent research has focussed upon notions taken from game theory, especially the theory of asymmetric information as well as the idea of principal–agent interaction. How much can they explain the puzzles of public administration and public management?
6   How is the recent emerging phenomena of multi-level governance analysed? It seems that understanding this requires not only theories of decentralisation or regionalisation but also network concepts.
7   What is the place of law in state management? An answer to this question requires reflection upon the rules-based nature of public organisation and governance as well as some insights into basic concepts in jurisprudence, such as rights, duties and competences.
8   Today the hottest topic is how to combine ecology and policy. A reply to this problem leads one to ponder over both empirical matters, i.e. how policy leads to pollution, and normative matters, i.e. what environmental principles should policies be based upon?
9   Finally, alternative country-specific models of effecting state management provide an interesting area for new research, posing questions as to why some countries have structured their public organisation in this way and not another, like other countries. Do outcomes differ with institutional set-ups?

This book offers an introduction to the research on these problematics. It is hoped that students may choose one or another theme in order to pursue more profound analyses than what can be done in this introductory text.

The public sphere: beyond the public and the private

State management or firm management, the public sector or the private sector, policy or market, nationalisation against privatisation – these are clear alternatives, it seems. Yet, following philosopher Habermas and his idea of the public sphere and sociologist Coleman with the notion of social capital, state management has begun to deliver policies in areas where there is considerable private ownership and initiative but also some key public dimension.

Post-NPM scholars argue that this grey zone between the public and the private, state and market, calls for a new kind of state management aiming at strengthening the so-called "public sphere", or maintaining social capital. Thus, for instance, government may be active in protecting cultural heritage, opening up access to cultural events for various groups of people including the physically challenged, although it may refrain from being the owner of cultural assets.

But, may one not retort that governments in their physical planning and urban policies already take into account the value of social capital? It seems that the new theme of the public sphere broadens the policy options for government, as it calls for government engagement in community matters, although there are other actors involved, such as civil society, private firms and single individuals.

In some of the advanced capitalist democracies, it is the local and regional governments that are responsible for many public services. Here, new institutional solutions in the last twenty years have resulted in the diversification of organisational forms. Thus, departments of local governments or bureaux of regional governments have engaged in interaction with an array of public and private organisations: collaboration but also competition.

This process of transforming the bureaucracies in the communes and county councils is referred to as the "externalisation of public service provision" (Thynne and Wettenhall, 2009). This outsourcing constitutes a challenge for local and regional government in combining managerial interests with political responsibility. The process of externalisation results in so-called networks between public and private actors that need coordination between the various stakeholders involved. Thynne and Wettenhall claim that important issues of ownership concerning the significance of "community" and "place" surface. What is clear is that a new form of management of public affairs, the governance of the public space, has appeared in some countries, but the link with ownership matters is not obvious.

The seminal trend in public sector reform in advanced countries has been an erosion of central government authority, the devolution of power and responsibility to decentralised levels of government and the introduction of managerialism and competition. The externalisation of public service provision in local and regional governments has changed the structure of government authority. The boundaries between the public and private sectors are increasingly rendered fuzzy due to the increase of interactions between so-called stakeholders. These major developments are analysed with concepts such as network government, New Public Management or the hollowing out of the state, depending upon from which perspective one starts. One may regard this new approach involving the governance of the public sphere or the public promotion of social capital as an attempt to recapture lost ground for state management after a decade or two of privatisation, hollowing out and downsizing of the state. Some scholars speak of new forms of public ownership of intangible assets like culture, community and solidarity. It remains to specify more in detail what this "ownership" really amounts to and how it differs from the standard regulatory tasks of any government in relation to the society or the "community".

Conclusion

State management is very different from private sector management. Examining the classical models of public administration, one would wish to insist upon the fact that public management is *sui generis*, meaning that it is not reducible to general management and its models of strategy, for instance. I would like to state a clear adherence to the difference hypothesis concerning public management. Its distinctive features set public management off from private management, including the dominant role of politics, the lack of proper ownership, the omnipresence of some kind of tax funding and the unmistakable format in the form of public law (Hood and Margetts, 2007).

There are a few major approaches to state management. They are so different that they should be analysed in comparison. They come down differently on the politics/administration divide that is so typical for public management in contradistinction to private management. In public administration for instance, politics has the upper hand with the call for neutral bureaucrats not to question policy. In public management as quangos or policy networks, managerialism prevails, as government is to be located at arm's length. In the policy framework, implementation becomes the missing link between legislation and outcomes. When public management is seen as marketisation, or tendering/bidding, then only the final responsibility for making sure that public services are forthcoming rests with government. Thus, even when the emphasis is strictly put upon getting the job done, politics is always present in public management somehow.

I firmly believe that the *difference hypothesis* is the correct one, stating that public management is different from private management. This entails that any direct transfer of managerialism from the private sector to the public sector is bound to fail, because managerialism does not pay enough attention to the aspects that derive from public organisation: laws, rule of law, budgeting and taxation, complaint and redress institutions (March and Olsen, 1989).

A theory of state management would do what the theory of management accomplishes for teaching in business schools around the world, namely, offer a comprehensive approach to how people are organised for the delivery of services to the population. It would comprise an assessment of the variety of models that the state can employ to get the job done. It outlines a distinct perspective upon government and its organisations.

Essential summary

1　A theory of state management would outline the key issues or problematics in the provision of public services.
2　State management differs from private sector management in several aspects, such as the role of taxation. One major difference is the strong rule of law requirement upon public management.
3　State management is intimately linked with public or administrative law, the implications of which used to be the major concern in the discipline of public administration.
4　State management theory faces a number of challenges, as the problematics in modelling public services provisions are numerous: degree of rationality, implementation gap or strategy, public–private partnerships or networks, New Public Management – outsourcing, incorporation, contracting in, the role of bureaucracies or other principal–agent mechanisms, the place of law and the role of regulation in governing the private sector, etc.
5　State management is fundamentally different from private firm management. This difference hypothesis may be supported in several ways.

Suggested readings

Bovaird, T. and E. Loeffler (2003) *Public Management and Governance.* London: Routledge.
Breton, A. (2007) *The Economic Theory of Representative Government.* New York: Aldine Transaction.
Cooper, P.J. and C.A. Newland (eds) (1977) *Handbook of Public Law and Administration.* San Francisco: Jossey-Bass.

Goodin, R.E. (2008) *The Theory of Institutional Design*. Cambridge: Cambridge University Press.

Gregory, B. (1989) "Political Rationality or 'Incrementalism'? Charles E. Lindblom's Enduring Contribution to Public Policymaking Theory", *Policy and Politics*, Vol. 17, No. 2: 139–153.

Hood, C.C. and H.Z. Margetts (2007) *The Tools of Government in the Digital Age*. Basingstoke: Palgrave Macmillan.

Hughes, O.E. (2003) *Public Management and Administration: An Introduction*. Basingstoke: Palgrave Macmillan.

Kelsen, H. (2005) *General Theory of Law and State*. Edison, NJ: Transaction Publishers.

Lane, J.-E. (2007) *Comparative Politics: The Principal–Agent Perspective*. London: Routledge.

Lindblom, C.E. and E.J. Woodhouse (1994) *The Policy Making Process*. Upper Saddle River, NJ: Pearson.

Loughlin, M. (2004) *The Idea of Public Law*. Oxford: Oxford University Press.

March, J.G. and J.P. Olsen (1989) *Rediscovering Institutions: Organisational Basis of Politics*. New York: Free Press.

Peters, B.G. and J. Pierre (eds) (2003) *Handbook of Public Administration*. London: SAGE Publications.

Rabin, J., W.B. Hildreth and G.J. Miller (eds) (1997) *Handbook of Public Administration*. New York: Marcel Dekker.

Thynne, I. and R. Wettenhall (eds) (2009) *Symposium on Ownership in the Public Sphere*, special issue of the *International Journal of Public Policy*.

Vincent, A. (1987) *Theories of the State*. Oxford: Blackwell.

Wildavsky, A (1987) *Speaking Truth to Power: Art and Craft of Policy Analysis*. Edison, NJ: Transaction Publishers.

Wildavsky, A. and N. Lynn (eds) (1990) *Public Administration: The State of the Discipline*. Chatham: Chatham House.

1 Formal organisation models

The relevance of informal organisation

Introduction

State management has often been constructed in terms of a naïve model of formal organisation, comprising little more than a chart outlining the various divisions, departments and supporting units. The basic assumption was that organisational behaviour tended to follow rules rather rigidly, so that the chart and its structure somehow corresponded to realities. However, this assumption was soon questioned as research got going within what is called public administration.

Public administration delivered a few models of public management that centred on formal organisation, reflecting the origin of this discipline within law, specifically, constitutional and administrative law. On the one hand, there was the positive Weberian or Wilsonian model of public management as bureaucracy. On the other hand, there was the critique of bureaucracy, stating basically that informal organisation tends to outweigh formal organisation.

This chapter argues against the *thesis of bureaucratic efficiency*, as the evidence is more in favour of the critique of bureaucracy than supporting the claim of the inherent efficiency of the bureau. Understanding public management requires much more than studying charts of formal organisation, however impressive they may look for big organisations.

The Weber or Wilson model

Max Weber in Germany and Woodrow Wilson in the United States both launched the model of the efficient bureau separately. Both adhered to the so-called politics/administration separation, searching for a structure of public management that would make it resist political incursions like favouritism. Formal organisation was seen as the method of achieving competent and neutral government in an era when large-scale organisations were coming forth in the private sector. The similarities between Weber, Wilson, Taylor and Fayol have often been pointed out, although the latter two concentrated upon the enterprise or private firms.

The classical model of bureaucracy harbours a theory of institutional features and their combined effect. The question is, of course, whether the model is based upon a correct hypothesis about institutions and their probable effects. Perhaps Weber was not entirely convinced himself, as he added another factor that would make bureaucracy operate in a satisfactory manner, namely, incentives in the form of the peculiar idea of vocation.

Wilson was very much at the head of the popular movement to clean up government in the United States, at all levels. What had to be contained was the principle of *spoils*, meaning that many positions in government were politically recruited and thus did not respect tenure. If the bureaucracy was to be recruited in an impartial manner with professional criteria only, then a theory of government was needed to say that administration could be separated from politics.

The model of the bureau as an efficient formal organisation is well-known: (1) hierarchy; (2) division of labour; (3) professional recruitment; (4) promotion based on seniority; (5) tenure; (6) discipline under predictable forms; (7) dismissal by means of court action (Weber, 1978).

Similar principles were advocated by Wilson and scientific management with Taylor and Fayol. This model of formal organisation has been applied in many governments: central, regional and local. And it sits well with administrative law where organisational charts could be added to the law text, delineating how the bureau would operate once it was funded.

Authorities, agencies and boards were organised according to this model. It seemed to fit the structural differentiation of universities into disciplines and the separation of health care specialities at hospitals. In local government, boards could be set up with both politicians and professional experts, being responsible for the delivery of one specified public service area. At the national government level, the model seemed almost a minutely detailed description of how ministries were operating, having their special functions executed within a structure of departments and subunits.

Both Weber and Fayol emphasised that formal organisation according to the model mentioned earlier (1–7) was what modernisation required, both in the public and the private sectors. When large-scale effort was needed, then bureaucracy was the answer to the search for efficiency.

Yet, the critique of the formal organisation model came rather soon, as it could also draw upon findings from private sector studies in the huge enterprises. All the variety of criticisms against the bureaucracy model had one idea in common: informal organisation cannot be bypassed, neither in public nor in private management.

The claims of the bureaucracy model

Public management involves bringing together a team of people and organising their work so that a set of objectives are promoted. It is small wonder that management study often goes under the name of "organisational analysis". The bureaucracy model sees organisation as mainly a question of structuring. If functions could be neatly separated in a strong division of labour and clear responsibility be allocated for these functions, then much of the management problem would have been resolved. The criticisms of the bureaucracy model targeted the following weaknesses:

1　Formal behaviour is not real behaviour; what actually happens may be very different from what the organisational chart intends.
2　Beneath formal organisation there always develops informal structures that may be highly important for results.
3　Formal organisation tends to be rigid in a way that is counterproductive for the achievement of goals.
4　The people at the top of the hierarchy may be less knowledgeable about practices than key so-called fixers far down in the structure.
5　Innovation may be critical for organisations facing a changing environment. But formal organisation does not automatically support innovation.

The bureaucracy model aims at securing an honest and efficient government, undoing all forms of appropriation of public resources – money, decisions, etc. The model is successful in promoting good governance, but will the bureau really be efficient?

Bureaucratic authority is based upon a belief in the correctness of the process by which administrative rules were enacted; the loyalty of the bureaucrat is oriented to an impersonal order, to a superior position. The following features characterise the employee as bureaucrat. First, mode of recruitment: the bureaucrat is not selected on the basis of such considerations as family position or political loyalties, but formal qualifications – diplomas, university degrees – that testify that the applicant has the necessary knowledge to accomplish his specialised duties effectively. Once a candidate enters the bureaucratic organisation, his office is his sole – or at least his primary – occupation. It constitutes a "career" with stability and continuity: a "life's work". Second, an elaborate system of remuneration and promotion: the principles of both seniority and achievement. The bureaucrat would normally receive a salary based not so much on his productivity performance as on the status of his position. Third, separation between the private and the public sphere of the bureaucrat's life: his private property is sharply distinguished from the "means of administration" that do not belong to him. Fourth, a system of control: based on rules for the whole organisation on the basis of technical knowledge and with the aim of achieving maximum efficiency. According to Weber, "Bureaucratic administration means fundamentally the exercise of control on the basis of knowledge. This is the feature of it which makes it specifically rational" (Weber, 1947: 339).

The model merely claims but never proves that its features guarantee maximum efficiency. Is bureaucracy specifically rational? Questioning this assumption leads one into the criticism of the formal organisation model, constituting a core theme in the discipline of organisation theory.

The critique of the bureaucracy model

Weber's emphasis upon bureaucracy as the basic model of managing government has been debated all along the rise of organisational sociology as a discipline. One may separate three counter-arguments:

(1) Bureaucracy leads to the bureaucratisation of society.

As an oligarchic system of domination, bureaucracy will sooner or later cease to be a tool for democracy. Instead it may become the master, the politically dominant group in a new type of society that is neither capitalist nor socialist. Michels was the first to model increasing bureaucratisation as an inherent oligarchic tendency in modern society. His model focussed on the internal political structure of large-scale organisations. His "iron law of oligarchy" postulates that with the increasing complexity and bureaucratisation of modern organisations all power is concentrated at the top, in the hands of an organisational elite that rules in a dictatorial manner.

Interestingly, the Italian Marxist Bruno Rizzi in *The Bureaucratisation of the World* (1939) presented an early argument that the huge bureaucracy in the newly formed Soviet Union had rapidly developed into a ruling class that could use the proletariat in much the same manner that capitalists did. In the Soviet system, the bureaucratic control of the means of production represented not "socialism" but "statism". The bureaucrats – technicians, directors, and specialists holding key positions in the party and state administration – would be inclined to steal the so-called surplus value of work. It was, however, Milovan Djilas with his *The New Class* (1957) who became world famous with a similar critique of the Yugoslav socialist regime.

It is often argued that bureaucracy is typical, not only of modern government, but also of the huge private corporation. James Burnham (1941) proposed a theory of the "managerial revolution" that was to be elaborated by John Galbraith. According to this theory, technological progress and large-scale economic growth has deprived the old capitalist class of capital owners of control of the means of production. Effective control of the economy has passed on to the managers, the new economic elite of CEOs (Burnham, 1972; Galbraith, 2007).

Argument (1) no doubt received its impetus from Weber's claim that not only should the state employ bureaucracy but also that the private sector would structure its large firms in that way. However, the organisation theory for private enterprises never fully endorsed formal organisation as the best tool for having efficient firms.

(2) Bureaucracy harbours pathologies.

Several American sociologists – Merton, Selznick, Gouldner and Etzioni – modelled how bureaucratic red tape and inefficiency surface sooner or later in formal organisation. The predominance of rational rules and their close control favours the reliability and predictability of the bureaucrat's behaviour, but it also accounts for his/her lack of flexibility and his/her tendency to turn means into ends. Indeed, the emphasis on strict observance of rules induces the individual to internalise them. Instead of simply being means, procedural rules become ends in themselves. "Goal displacement" occurs, as the instrumental and formalistic aspect of the bureaucratic role becomes more important than the substantive one, the achievement of the main organisational goals. A bureaucratic feature such as strict control by rules can both promote and hinder organisational efficiency, having both functional effects, such as predictability and precision, and dysfunctional effects, such as rigidity. Some theorists have rejected the functional approach, contending that organisations must be seen as configurations of antagonistic groups that aim to promote their conflicting interests. Bureaucracies tend to suboptimise results or outcomes.

(3) Bureaucracy, first and foremost, harbours power.

This is the argument of French sociologist M. Crozier. Bureaucracy is modelled by him as centres where power is sought after and becomes a source of conflict. When Crozier started his research into the French social structure of the industrial society after the Second World War – Crozier carried out his first research in 1953 on the white-collar workers in the French Postal Bank – it comprised cohesive and often hostile occupational groups. These groups would focus upon the rules of interaction, i.e. the norms for both action within the groups and between the groups. Rules of interaction limit arbitrariness in both ordinary life and within organisations. Yet, rules do not cover everything, meaning that uncertainty leads to conflicts out of which direct dominance and subordination develop. Crozier's basic idea was that groups controlling this unregulated area possess a strategic advantage to be used to capture organisational rewards.

Invited in 1959 to the Center for Advanced Study in the Behavioral Sciences, Crozier drafted *The Bureaucratic Phenomenon*. It established the sociology of organisations as a discipline in France, sketching out the basis of what would later on become the "strategic analysis of organisations". In 1977, Crozier and Erhard Friedberg published *L'Acteur et le système (Actors and Systems*, 1981), which outlines an approach to the study of both organisations and less formalised systems of action. Organisations operate within game structures that channel bargaining relations between interdependent actors, resulting in power. Not only the rules of the game matter, but especially important is how the players develop strategies in relation to the rules, which are often opaque or ambiguous. Often the institutions constrain more than they liberate human energies.

The bureaucracy model has been a core element in the discipline of public administration. Within public administration there has been a long and profound debate about the pros and cons of the Weber–Wilson model. Public administration as a discipline is not monolithic but harbours a variety of views. Thus, after the Second World War, Waldo questioned the efficiency claims of the bureaucracy model in his painstaking critique of the formal organisation model. And Appleby rejected the validity of the politics/administration distinction. Yet, the public administration school today defends the formal organisation model, stating that bureaucracy is still very much relevant to public management, and that the critique of bureaucracy lacks empirical evidence.

The public administration rebuttal

The endorsement of bureaucracy as the model of public management has come from public administration scholars such as Goodsell (2003) and Fredrickson (1996). Goodsell argues that American public servants and administrative institutions generate social capital. Contrary to the stereotypes disseminated by the public choice school and laissez-faire economists, they are hardly sources of great waste and do not constitute a real threat to liberty. Civil servants in operation supply social assets of critical value to democracy. Thus, Goodsell contradicts the image of public bureaucracy that has spread in the wake of Thatcherism and Reaganomics.

The message given by popular literature regarding government bureaucracy is rejected by several public administration experts as one-sided. The surge of New Right literature from many so-called think tanks reinforced the overall characterisation of government bureaucracy within the popular image of it being overstaffed, inflexible, unresponsive and power hungry. The free market economists are hostile to government bureaucracy on the basis that competitive markets and profit incentives are the best means to obtain efficiency. Many sociologists have been more concerned with the pathologies of bureaucracy and several political scientists more inclined to underline its monopoly or oligopoly features than simply defending an institution that delivers services in well-ordered societies in a predictable and just manner. Thus, to Goodsell, the criticism of bureaucracy is not well supported by empirical data. According to him, the success of bureaucracy is mainly limited by ambiguous goals given to the bureaucracy, the recent problem of coordination created by excessive outsourcing, administration by proxy, and the growing complexity of societal problems that government is confronting. Goodsell's favourable evaluation of bureaucracy contrasts with that of Crozier but is in line with the views of many American public administration scholars, especially from the Maxwell School of Syracuse University.

The third view: bureaucracy as a balanced organisation

If one wishes to read a modern Weberian appreciation of formal organisation, then one should turn to *Bureaucracy: What Government Agencies Do and Why They Do It* (1991) by J.Q. Wilson. It is widely considered a most comprehensive and strongly supported enquiry into federal agencies from the empirical point of view. The book, which deviates markedly from the economic or rational choice approaches to bureaucracy with, for example, Downs (1993), is structured into: organisations, operators, managers, executives, context and change. Wilson's thesis that organisation matters entails that the team of employees must be lined up in accordance with the objectives of the agency. Is bureaucracy capable of efficiency, i.e. achieving the objectives fully while minimising operative costs?

Efficiency in a bureaucracy has two aspects, namely, inner efficiency or productivity, as well as outer efficiency or effectiveness. The behaviour of the operators – street-level bureaucrats – and their culture would be shaped by the imperatives of the situation they encounter on a daily basis. The managers of public agencies have to focus their attention upon these two constraints, derived from the objectives as well as the situational exigencies. The norm of efficiency may be endangered, as the executives of government agencies compete with other departments and they employ strategies in the process of competition and/or cooperation – the generation of turf.

The context in which public agencies do their business is distinctly political: Congress, the president and courts, in the case of the US. Wilson classifies government agencies into four groups: production organisations, procedural organisations, craft organisations and coping organisations. This distinction is chiefly based upon the visibility/measurability of the organisations' outputs and procedures. The "production organisation" has both measurable processes and visible/understandable outputs (i.e. Social Security Administration). "Procedural organisations" perform measurable processes, but they have no visible or easily measurable outputs. The "craft organisation" is characterised by having immeasurable processes and visible outputs (i.e. the armies). However, the "coping organisation" has neither measurable/controllable processes nor visible outputs (i.e. the Police Department, the Department of Education).

Wilson approaches public sector productivity in an unusual manner: if normal productivity (inner efficiency) is the ratio of input to output, then can the outputs of bureaux be measured/quantified? He argues that "contextual goals" sought by public organisations, in addition to their main objectives, may make the efficiency measurement problem opaque. If contextual goals are taken into consideration, then the efficiency of the public organisation may be evaluated more positively. But what is the mission of a bureaucracy?

To Wilson, the mission of an organisation is the same as the public agency's culture, when its culture is widely shared among most of the organisation's members. Connecting mission to culture is crucial in the public sector, as the culture of public agencies helps to define their mission. Culture comes forth according to the situational mandates of the work being done. Yet, if reform of a bureaucracy is to be feasible, it must take into account the situational imperatives of the public sector organisations, and the reward system must be suitable to the output expected, overcoming resistance to change, so typical of bureaux.

Public agencies are often not given specific and well-defined goals due to the multiplication of interests. According to Wilson, as time passes, different interests find a place in the mission of the organisation and accordingly, new goals are added to the list of "objectives" of the agency that may be contradictory to each other.

The key problem: when to employ bureaucracy?

One line of defence of the bureaucratic mode of organisation is to relate organisation to context. Thus, Mintzberg (1997) identified five chief organisational structures: (1) The Simple Structure, (2) Machine Bureaucracy, (3) Professional Bureaucracy, (4) The Divisionalised Form, and (5) The Adhocracy. And he argued a well-known thesis that stable organisational environments with a high degree of certainty in the technology employed favoured the bureaucracy whereas rapidly changing situations called for other modes of organisation – at least when it came to the structure of the firm or enterprises. Similar arguments were voiced in the so-called contingency school of organisational theory (Donaldson, 2001). However, they theorise the advantages and disadvantages of bureaucracy in private enterprises. Things are somewhat different in public organisations since they are not profit maximisation organisations.

The frequent use of bureaucracy in the state is at least partly to be explained by two other reasons. First, we have the rule of law reason. Even when it is true that bureaucracies operate slowly, do not maximise output and are not always consumer friendly, they tend to respond to a variety of requirements that the rule of law regime calls for. Thus, bureaucracies respect the principles of handling a so-called *dossier*, i.e. it keeps all the records concerning a case and invites the people concerned to file a complaint, if they wish to. Thus, there are mechanisms to allow for *voice*, i.e. grievances and compensation, in the bureaucracy, following the principle that it should be possible to attack all decisions concerning a *dossier*.

Second, we have organisations where coordination consists mainly in respect of each subunit, for instance, universities. When the basis of an organisation is to be found with highly autonomous production units, living, so to speak, their own lives, bureaucracy offers a strong protection for integrity and professionalism. Universities could not possibly be governed in any way other than bureaucracy.

Bureaucracy offers protection for the civil servants and professionals who work there in several ways. It is not only a matter of job security, or tenure, but the protection offered by this institutional mechanism covers beliefs and values also. Thus, bureaucrats are not merely supposed to be loyal to their masters, but they may also speak the truth to those in power. Some bureaucracies like universities and research units are so separated from the daily world of politics and business that they almost have a complete life of their own.

The modernisation of formal organisation: decentralisation, deconcentration and devolution

One of the major reform efforts during the last twenty years has been to make formal organisation more efficient. Several countries have conducted reforms aiming at the decentralisation of the bureaucratic apparatus of the state. This is *not* the same as New Public Management, as it aims to change bureaucracy and not to undo it.

The surfeit of attention given to NPM – marketisation, privatisation, incorporation – has led to a neglect of the many efforts to modernise the state through making its formal organisation more effective and citizen responsive. It is still the case that bureaucracy is the predominant model of organising public employees. Thus, decentralisation has meant that a majority of public employees now work for regional or local governments. Decentralisation has offloaded the central government while at the same time strengthening democracy by empowering regional or local assemblies as democratically elected bodies.

Take, for instance, Denmark: through the structural reform that came into operation as of 1 January 2007, the number of local governments (municipalities) was reduced from 271 to 98. Similarly, the number of counties was reduced from 13 to 5 new regions. The basic motive behind the structural reform was to increase government capacity. Thus, the average number of inhabitants in local governments will now be much higher, at around 55,000 inhabitants. Local governments have taken over some responsibility for peripheral health matters, while the hospitals are the main activity of the new regions.

The division of tasks between regional and local governments is an ongoing concern in the politics of decentralisation. In some countries, the regional level has been strengthened while in others it has been weakened. Thus, in the Scandinavian countries the power of local governments has increased at the expense of regional ones. It seems that the opposite has occurred in Southern Europe and France. In a rather spectacular reform, the Norwegian government nationalised the hospitals, stripping the regional governments of functions and resources, which suggests that centralisation is also conceivable as a form of state innovation.

When the central government moves functions from the central level to its regional or local state offices, then we speak of "deconcentration". Many governments, for instance, have moved bureaucrats from the capital to the province(s) in an effort to off-load the centre and stimulate regional development. Thus, ministries have shed functions and labour to regional or local state offices in an effort to deconcentrate central state administration. E-governance opens up many possibilities to move functions out of large ministries, as civil servants and public employees can do their work over a terminal at some local office or even at home.

State modernisation may also involve the creation of regions with special competences, as with devolution in the UK, resulting in different structures in Scotland, Wales and Northern Ireland. Such asymmetrical state modernisation is also to be found in Spain, which raises the question of the possibilities of blending unitarism and federalism.

Bureaucracy: a second-best organisation?

The bureaucratic efficiency hypothesis cannot be upheld, given all the research during the twentieth century into formal organisation and hierarchy. However, one could argue that bureaucracy is a second-best institution, at least within the public sector. A second-best hypothesis would focus upon a trade-off between efficiency and rule of law, with formal organisation and hierarchy scoring high on the latter but low or medium on the former.

To score high on rule of law, the state would need, first and foremost, formal organisation oriented towards the enforcement of rules. Hierarchy may be highly instrumental for the purpose of having clear lines of responsibility and avenues for complaint. This is a different logic from that of efficiency or productivity, which targets the production of outputs and outcomes.

Thus, when state management is reformed along lines suggested by the so-called NPM philosophy, then care must be taken to preserve the rule of law framework for all kinds of public services. It happens of course that one forgets about the rule of law implications for the delivery of public services, moving too quickly to adopt an alternative institutional arrangement that scores higher than bureaucracy on effectiveness/productivity.

Bureaucracy still appears to be the most suitable organisation for the delivery of public services that pertain very much to the rule of law, such as the police, the military, the judiciary and the university. Due to the implications of these services for personal security, the employment of force and the pursuit of truth and justice, the delivery of them is bound to be highly restrained by rules and regulation. Of course, these organisations may also wish to employ institutions other than bureaucracy for certain parts of their activities, but not in relation to their core operations.

E-governance

The advantages or disadvantages of institutions such as bureaucracy change with advances in technology. The arrival of electronic media for transmitting information is about to change the way government goes about its business. Information is a central aspect of government operations, either internally or externally, with the population or other governments. The internet revolution has made information much cheaper, which has tremendous implications for the public sector and its organisation. Just to take some examples: citizens may be informed about their pensions, or the pension that may be expected for the future, by simply logging onto a website. Future employees may apply for a job by means of their email. Finally, the memory of a country as hosted in its libraries may to a considerable extent be available directly on the Web, to be downloaded by any user anywhere.

The idea of e-governance is still in the making. Thus, one speculates about the possibility of reforming democracy by e-voting: how is it made safe and cost efficient? For public administration, the arrival of e-governance reduces the relevance of the bureaucracy model. Recalling the ideal-type features of the Weberian model of formal organisation, the usefulness of hierarchy and division of labour is decreased by the internet revolution. Information can be stored and worked upon at lower levels in the organisation and it becomes easier for one person to handle several tasks quickly. E-governance makes public organisation more open and responsive to citizens as well as more accessible for governments. Two consequences are conceivable from the internet and information revolution:

1   Bureaucracies transform themselves by integrating the implication of the information revolution into their operating procedures – like the post-modern flat organisation.
2   Bureaucracies are replaced by more efficient organisations, public or private.

The theory of the post-bureaucratic organisation integrates the internet revolution and its implications for government. One may argue that Clinton's reinvention of government reform was to some extent an attempt to adapt the Washington bureaucracies to a post-modern image of a flexible, flat, efficient knowledge organisation (Heeks, 2001; Milner, 2000).

UNESCO has made a few valuable distinctions concerning the concept. Thus, the goals of e-governance may be to enable better organisation of governments' internal processes, or promote more efficient delivery of services and information, or enhance transparency, legitimacy and accountability in the public sector. UNESCO sets out three fields of implementation for achieving these goals in relation to the use of information and communication technologies (ICT):

1   *e-administration* – effectively, e-government that uses ICT to create more efficacious management of governmental policies and practices;
2   *e-services* – the evolution and sustenance of interactively accessed public services;
3   *e-democracy* – active and direct engagement of all citizens in the political process and the management of governmental outcomes.

(Budd, 2008: 98)

Thus far, the evaluation of e-governance policies indicate that results come easier in the first two areas cited (1 and 2) (Budd and Harris, 2008), but also that the expectations on DEG (Digital Era Governance) have been exaggerated.

The flat post-bureaucratic organisation

"Post-bureaucratic" is a word used for a range of ideas developed since the 1980s that contrast with Weber's ideal-type bureaucracy, including Total Quality Management, Culture Management and the Matrix Organisation amongst others. None of these replace the core tenets of bureaucracy:

hierarchies, authority and formal organisation. Some theorists have suggested a theory of a post-bureaucratic organisation (Heckscher and Donnellon, 1994), describing an organisation with an alternative institutional set-up. In such an ideal-type organisation, decisions are based on dialogue and consensus rather than authority and command, and the organisation is a network rather than a hierarchy, open at the boundaries. Still others are developing an interest in so-called complexity theory, spelling out its implications for the structuring of organisations. They focus on how simple structures can be used to engender organisational adaptations, as simple structures could generate new outcomes in, for instance, product development.

The Heckscher and Donnellon model would target the generation of trust within a post-bureaucratic organisation: information technology, horizontal and vertical information-sharing, multi-level consensus, partnerships across boundaries and negotiated solutions, as well as new managerial roles – as change agent, coordinator, broker and boundary-crosser. Is it equally applicable in private firms as to public organisations?

The search for alternatives to bureaucracy may be driven by two different reasons. On the one hand, there is the constant drive for better productivity and effectiveness with organisations delivering public services – the economic rationale. On the other hand, there is the new emphasis upon trust, or social capital. Organisations, from the micro to the macro, deliver better – it is claimed – when the employees relate to each other on the basis of trust, bringing forth natural spontaneous cooperation. Perhaps trust is more omnipresent in the flat post-bureaucratic organisation than in the traditional hierarchy?

The transformation of local authorties and bureaucracies

The local (and regional) governments used to be bureaucratic authorities in European countries, where local (and regional) government is responsible for education, health care, water supply, sewage, waste disposal, streets, harbours, social care, etc. Grossi *et al.* (2009) show that these subnational governments have recently undergone important changes, extensive public sector reform, transforming these bureaucratic hierarchies. Local (and regional) governments provided a number of vital services, using a carpet of bureaux, governed by a board of politicians. The transformation of the local governments for example in Sweden and Italy involve the "externalisation" of local public service provision through various forms of incorporation, public–public collaboration, public–private partnerships, and contracting out. So-called externalisation has changed local public service provision arrangements. Local governments in several countries now exercise their authority by cooperating or competing with an array of public and private providers.

Managerial reforms inspired by New Public Management have spread private sector managerial tools and principles to both central and local governments, with the objective of obtaining greater effectiveness, efficiency and economy. Institutional reforms have reduced the role of central government in the economic field through the devolution of power and responsibilities to decentralised levels of government, as well as through privatisation.

Local and regional governments in various countries have gradually abandoned direct forms of management in favour of more indirect forms. These non-bureaucratic forms of management comprise the transformation of units within local and regional governments into semi-autonomous organisations with (mostly) their own legal status based on private law concepts and with considerable managerial freedom; inter-municipal arrangements of joint service delivery, along with the establishment of contractual or institutional public–private partnerships (PPPs), contracting-out, and the delegation of service delivery power to private for-profit and non-profit organisations; and the total transfer of ownership and/or certain functions and services to private companies.

With the objective of providing better quality services to citizens in a more competitive environment, Italian and Swedish local governments, for instance, have been involved in various forms of so-called externalisation. This externalised, more private-law form of organisation with lots of incorporation, especially with regard to the management of business services – electricity, gas, water, waste disposal and public transport – has been driven by the objective of having organisations with more autonomy from the local or regional governments (Grossi *et al.*, 2009).

Conclusion

The formal organisation model has long dominated thinking about public management. It was applied by governments when setting up and running bureaucracies. However, its theoretical credentials turned out to be more and more criticised, as research into organisations developed in the twentieth century.

The pros and cons of public management as bureaucracy are still hotly debated. Those in favour emphasise the stability of bureaucracy and its contribution to the rule of law by underlining legality of operations. Others are more negative, linking bureaucracy with profound principal–agent difficulties and a tendency towards pathology (Brunsson and Olsen, 1993). But public management has moved away from the classical model of bureaucracy, as governments have searched for new methods of service production and delivery. Bureaucracy is still greatly used in public management, but it is far from being the sole model. The public administration school still maintains that bureaucracy offers a balanced organisation, but in New Public Management bureaucracy is bypassed by resorting to other modes of organisation.

Theoretically, the bureaucracy model did not only make unwarranted claims about its performance, but it also left out many aspects of public management. Basic questions about incentives were left unanswered in the formal organisation or bureaucracy school (Ostrom, 2006). It should be pointed out that bureaucracy is still much employed by governments to get the job done. Few countries have gone so far as the UK to demolish formal organisation, replacing it with contracts and public–private partnerships. It involves perhaps a misrepresentation that so much of the new literature on public management deals with the UK, as most other countries have not followed the "third way".

If government is looked upon as the principal of the public sector, then it may choose among different agents to get the job done, bureaucracy constituting only one such mechanism. Thus, alternative governance structures may be analysed as different ways of government contracting with agents and monitoring their performance.

Essential summary

1 Formal organisation, or a set of bureaux, is a major element in state management, but scholars disagree about the nature of bureaucracy.
2 The classical analysis of Weber stated the positive argument for using bureaucracy for the tasks of state management.
3 The critique of Weber has resulted in a wide spectrum of arguments against formal organisation, more or less radical in tone.
4 Public sector reform in the last twenty years has come up with a number of ways to make bureaux more responsive to people's demands and more effective or productive, leading to the search for the post-bureaucratic organisation.
5 The standard reforms of formal organisation include *inter alia*: decentralisation, deconcentration, devolution and e-governance.
6 Some countries have ventured the NPM philosophy, restructuring bureaucracy completely – "externalisation".
7 The problem of bureaucracy – instructing, motivating and monitoring public employees in formal organisations – belongs under the principal–agent gaming.

Suggested readings

Brunsson, N. (1998) *Organising Organisations*. Copenhagen: Copenhagen Business School Press.

Brunsson, N. and J.P. Olsen (1993) *The Reforming Organisation*. London: Routledge.

Budd, L. (2008) "The Limits of Post-Lisbon Governance in the European Union", in L. Budd and L. Harris (eds) *e-Governance: Managing or Governing?* London: Routledge, 92–122.

Budd, L. and L. Harris (2008) *e-Governance: Managing or Governing?* London: Routledge.

Burnham, J. (1972) *The Managerial Revolution*. Westport, CT: Greenwood Press.

Crozier, M. (1981) *L'acteur et le système: les contraintes de l'action collective*. Paris: Seuil.

Crozier, M. (1971) *Le phénomène bureaucratique*. Paris: Seuil.

Donaldson, L. (2001) *The Contingency Theory of Organisations*. London: Sage Publications.

Downs, A. (1993) *Inside Bureaucracy*. Long Grove, IL: Waveland.

Dunleavy, P., H. Margetts, S. Bastow and J. Tinkler (2006) "New Public Management is Dead – Long Live Digital Era Governance", *Journal of Public Administration Research and Theory*, Vol. 16: 467–494.

Frederickson, H.G. (1996) *The Spirit of Public Administration*. San Francisco: Jossey-Bass.

Fredrickson, H.G. and K.B. Smith (2003) *Public Administration Theory Primer*. Boulder, CO: Westview Press.

Galbraith, J.K. (2007) *The New Industrial State*. Princeton: Princeton University Press.

Goodsell, C.T. (2003) *The Case for Bureaucracy: A Public Administration Polemic*. Washington, DC: CQ Press, U.S.

Gregory, R. (2008) "New Public Management and the Politics of Accountability", in S. Goldfinch and J. Wallis (eds) *International Handbook of Public Sector Reform*. London: Edward Elgar.

Gregory, R. (2007) "New Public Management and the Ghost of Max Weber: Exorcised or Still Haunting?", in T. Christensen and P. Laegreid (eds) *Transcending New Public Management: The Transformation of Public Sector Reforms*. Aldershot, UK: Ashgate.

Grossi, G., D. Argento, T. Tagesson and S.-O. Collin (2009) "The 'Externalisation' of Local Public Service Delivery: Experience in Italy and Sweden", in I. Thynne and R. Wettenhall (eds) (2009) *Symposium on Ownership in the Public Sphere*, special issue of the *International Journal of Public Policy*.

Heckscher, C. and A. Donnellon (eds) (1994) *The Post-Bureaucratic Organisation: New Perspectives on Organisational Change*. London: Sage.

Heeks, R. (ed.) (2001) *Reinventing Government in the Information Age: International Practice in IT-Enabled Public Sector Reform*. London: Routledge.

Hirschman, A.O. (1999) *Exit, Voice and Loyalty: Responses to Decline in Firms, Organizations and States.* Cambridge, MA: Harvard University Press.

Milner, E. (2000) *Managing Information and Knowledge in the Public Sector.* London: Routledge.

Mintzberg, H. (1997) *Structure in Fives: Designing Effective Organisations.* New York: Prentice Hall.

Ostrom, V. (2006) *The Intellectual Crisis in American Public Administration.* Tuscaloosa, AL: University of Alabama Press.

Rhodes, R.A.W., S.A. Binder and B.A. Rockman (eds) (2006) *The Oxford Handbook of Political Institutions.* Oxford: Oxford University Press.

Waldo, D. (2006) *The Administrative State: A Study of the Political Theory of American Public Administration.* H.T. Miller (Introduction). Edison, NJ: Transaction Publishers.

Weber, M. (1978) *Economy and Society.* Berkeley: University of California Press.

Weber, M. (1947) *The Theory of Social and Economic Organisation.* New York: Free Press.

Wilson, J.Q. (1991) *Bureaucracy: What Government Agencies Do and Why They Do It.* New York: Basic Books.

Web resources

http://en.wikipedia.org/wiki/Robert_Michels (last accessed on 1/11/2008).

http://www.marxists.org/archive/rizzi/bureaucratisation/index.htm (last accessed on 1/11/2008).

http://en.wikipedia.org/wiki/Milovan_Djilas (last accessed on 1/11/2008).

2 Asymmetric information models

The principal–agent perspective

Introduction

Public sector reform everywhere broke up the monolithic nature of the public sector. As a result of deconcentration, decentralisation, incorporation, internal markets, quangos and policy networks, the public sector displays a rich variety of governance structures. When social insurance is added to the picture, then complexity increases again with new ideas about workfare state, etc. Can this heterogeneity be captured in terms of one model? Yes, the principal–agent framework from institutional economics and the economics of information amounts to an attempt to do just that.

Agency theory is popular within both corporate governance and public management. One party as a principal hires someone else, an agent, to do work against compensation. The pay will come out of the result that the agent creates. Thus, in this interaction there is both cooperation, i.e. how to get the best results possible, and conflict, i.e. how to divide the resulting gains. Principal–agent interaction is basically a contractual issue: how to strike bargains and how to monitor them when they enter into effect.

The principal–agent model was first employed in insurance in modelling the interaction between the insured person and the company offering insurance. Then it was used to understand the problem in agriculture, whether to employ farm labour or engage in sharecropping. Finally, it was realised that paying the CEO of a company amounts to solving a principal–agent problem, where alternative strategies on the part of the principal result in different outcomes for the agent. Of course, it was only a matter of time until it was realised that public management is to a large extent a host of principal–agent relationships.

Contracting with agents

The principal–agent model covers in principle all kinds of contractual relationships where government – central, regional or local – asks someone or a team of people, whatever their organisational framework may be, to take part in delivering public services. Thus, one may analyse both bureaucracy and internal markets within this approach. The key idea is that making contracts that last longer than so-called spot-on contracts opens up the possibility for contractual opportunism, whether it is a matter of a contract in the public or private sectors. Besides the problem of arriving at Pareto-optimal contracts, there is the hiatus between the *ex ante* contract and the *ex post* contract. How is contractual fulfilment monitored?

The government as principal is assumed to be wholly preoccupied with politics and policy. It needs lots of people to get things done, meaning, from organisation to the delivery of services. It makes no difference whether government uses its own people or relies upon people from the private sector or the third sector (people working in third sector organisations or voluntary non-profit organisations). Delivering services remains a question of how much to pay for what result, taking into account the occurrence of agent opportunism in the interaction with his/her principal.

"Opportunism" stands for all kinds of strategies that a person may engage in for the purpose of gaining more than what is regular. The principal–agent framework targets asymmetric information, which is a technical term in game theory referring to situations where one actor does not know all the alternatives of action. More specifically, he/she does not know where he/she is placed in a game tree, or who the other actor is. There are two kinds of asymmetric information in principal–agent games, *moral hazard* on the one hand and *adverse selection* on the other. In moral hazard, the agent changes his/her behaviour after the contract. In adverse selection, the principal does not know with which type of agent he/she is contracting.

It may sound startling to discuss public service delivery as a host of contractual matters. After all, contract law belongs to private law and contracting is analysed in microeconomics, which deals with consumer choice and producer strategy. Although the state rests upon authority and law, government cannot normally order people to work for it but must contract. It may use long-term contracts, as in various forms of tenure, or it may buy the provision of services for a short time duration, as in various tendering/bidding schemes.

Opportunism in contracting takes the form of either reneging or pretending. It results in inefficiencies from which one of the parties, i.e. the agent, stands to gain. Reneging often occurs in contracting, as when one party deliberately manoeuvres away from the fulfilment of the terms of the contract. It may be done explicitly on one occasion or slowly over a longer period of time on another. Pretending occurs before the contract is concluded, when an agent hides his/her true nature, signing up to a contract that he/she cannot deliver. One could say that *ex ante* opportunism amounts to lying whereas *ex post* opportunism implies cheating. To fully understand the economics of information and its emerging principal–agent framework, one must focus upon the concept of effort and its consequences.

Effort in the agency relationship

In the principal–agent model of contracting, the key entity is called "effort". It denotes much more, as it covers all characteristics of an agent that are relevant when making the contract: willingness to work, capacity to work, experience, skills, education, etc. It is effort that explains why contractual failures occur.

Theoretically speaking, output depends upon effort, and the value of output is used to pay for the agent. One may assume only two levels of effort in order to arrive at the theoretical implications, high and low, where opportunism is employed for the capturing of a rent. Thus, one has the following model:

Table 2.1 Expected value in a principal–agent model

	Output	
	Small = 100	*High = 500*
Low Effort	0.8	0.2
High Effort	0.2	0.8

Since the expected value of low effort is 180, compared to the expected value of high effort at 420, the principal would want the agent to be a high effort agent. This ambition comes, however, with a higher price tag, as the agent responds to incentive compatibility and demands higher pay for higher effort. The agent would in any case want to be paid the reservation price whether he/she put in low or high effort.

The solution of the game – effort against remuneration – is highly unstable, because there may be asymmetric information. The outcome depends not only upon the number of agents available or the number of principals looking for agents, but also upon strategy on the part of the agent: moral hazard or adverse selection. When contractual opportunism occurs either before or after the contract, then the principal may stand to lose considerably, especially when contracting for high effort but receiving low effort.

Moral hazard is a well-known phenomenon in public management, but under other labels. Terms such as "slack", "bureau waste", "red tape" and "X-inefficiency" refers to the same phenomenon. Well-known models for the public sector such as Parkinson's bureau growth and Niskanen's budget maximising are fundamentally moral hazard models, although not presented in terms of the principal–agent approach.

Adverse selection occurs in the hiring process of workers or managers, in both the private and the public sector. Screening is most often employed in order to separate agents, but there exist other strategies as well. When public management adopts contracting out or in, then it is likely that adverse selection surfaces as the major difficulty. Contractual mistakes tend to be costly to correct, as transaction costs start outpacing the gains in production from internal market schemes.

Teams and team production

One may analyse organisational structure as principal–agent links, going from the owner of the organisation over higher and middle level managers to the white- and blue-collar workers. In public organisations like bureaux and agencies, the owner is the legal person that we call the "state", and government is its representative. Thus, from government flows the principal–agent links downwards in the hierarchy. Under the principal–agent framework, there is no difference between agents organised as a bureau or agency and agents organised as joint-stock companies. They are all teams of people with whom two kinds of contracts may be entered into in the governance relationship:

1 the team contract
2 the individual team member contract.

With the principal–agent framework, the first contract will specify the output of the team as well as its remuneration. The real contract will reflect bargaining power among principals and agents as well as the probability of strategies like moral hazard and adverse selection. The second contract will be made by the team itself, deliberating over the value of the contribution of each individual employee to the final team product. Ideally, managers would like to set the wage where the marginal value of the contribution to the team of each employee is, but it is impossible for monitoring reasons, given the ever present danger of asymmetric information, i.e. moral hazard and adverse selection.

The basic problem of teams in the public sector can be stated in the following manner, focussing here upon in-house production. Whether the principal employs bureaucracy or quangos, he/she would want to maximise the gain G from operating certain activities A, resulting in output O. However, the team must be paid a remuneration W for its effort E. Thus, we have:

1 $O = A + \epsilon$ (error)
2 $A = E$, whether HE (high effort) or LE (low effort)

3   W = S + b (wage equals salary plus bonus)
4   S = A, given that S > agent's reservation price
5   G = O – W – FC (gain is output minus wage minus fixed costs).

The principal would wish to maximise G, subject to agency costs. Thus, he/she would attempt to find an incentive scheme that maximises output while minimising agency costs. In the private sector, the wage may include a big bonus (b) part (b > 0 <1), or the salary S may be linked with some objective criterion such as hours worked, or a subjective criterion such as reputation. It is in principle impossible to link the salary with effort, since it is considered neither observable nor verifiable. Thus, a contract based upon effort levels (low or high) between a principal and a team would invite opportunism on both sides, resulting in reneging, reply and retaliation (Gibbons, 1998).

For the governance of public teams, things become in practice more difficult, as it is messy to operate a bonus system (b) when the output has no market value. Thus, besides the unobservable and unverifiable component of team effort (E), there is the problem of the immeasurability of the value of the output to the principal. Incentive schemes for teams will be composed of a variety of indicators of team output, productivity and capacity. Thus, incentives have been linked with: (1) standard input of hours; (2) age or seniority; (3) assessments of competence; (4) sharing of yearly surpluses; (5) monitoring of individual contribution. The problem of team governance may be resolved by a mixture of two extreme solutions: tenure on the one hand and remuneration by hour on the other hand.

Principal–agent framework of state management

In my view, the principal–agent approach is the only conceptual framework that may cover both public management and public administration. It is also applicable to the analysis of networks and may be broadened from strict economist concerns to also include trust and the building up of social capital between government and service providers.

Government as the principal of the public sector may employ a variety of agents under alternative governance structures. Bureaucracy is merely one such type of agent, i.e. an agent with a long-term contract with government. Short-term employment of agents is favoured within New Public Management. NPM stands for the many public sector reforms initiated in the 1980s and pushed through in the 1990s. It covers decentralisation, empowerment of lower echelons and the internal market schemes. These reforms, albeit very different in nature and consequences, were much inspired by agency theory and economics.

As the public sector kept expanding every year at a quicker pace than overall GDP growth, a critique of big government emerged that focussed upon the increase in the number of public employees and bureaux. The public choice school and its message, particularly adamant about the growth of bureaucracies, had an influence upon politicians facing ever bigger deficits. The Weberian philosophy of bureaucracy as efficiency was replaced by a suspicion that the bureaux as agents played games with their principals and got away with them. Strategy became a major concern with politicians, who had for a long period of time accepted public sector growth. According to agency theory, the only remedy would be choice and competition among agents.

Downsizing the bureaux at various levels of government could be done by contracting out. Thus, the Next Steps Initiative was born in the UK, which introduced so-called executive agencies into Whitehall, and the Reinventing Government programme in Washington, DC. And in the Nordic countries the internal markets were introduced, sometimes entirely replacing formal organisation with bureaux, especially at local and regional government levels.

On the one hand, NPM favoured schemes that allowed for some form of tendering/bidding, meaning short-term contracts and contracting out. Sometimes this ambition was carried to extremes, such as when private firms took over government financial records and auditing. Often public employees would quit the bureau and organise themselves privately, just to bid for the delivery of public services. Thus, public employment decreased but the number of people contracted with exploded. Critics called this process of downsizing the "hollowing out" of the state. The reduction of bureaucrats in Whitehall as well as in Washington, DC, was quite substantial. As soon as public management turns to various schemes for short-term contracting on a large scale, it faces the adverse selection problem. Nowhere was this clearer than in the developments in New Zealand. Public procurement is less vulnerable to adverse selection than internal market schemes, because competition is more naturally forthcoming.

On the other hand, public administration harbours the moral hazard problem, which Weber failed to pin down or address properly. Weber addressed one aspect of the principal–agent difficulties, i.e. moral hazard in long-term contracting, by throwing in *Deux ex Machina*, namely, vocation being the driving motivation of bureaucrats. Bureaux and agencies have an information advantage that they tend to employ for capturing a rent. It is the size of this rent that politicians and bureaucrats or professionals tend to fight about, engaging in alternative strategies and using different institutions. It remains to develop principal–agent theory for networks and public–private partnerships, modelling how principals and agents may generate trust, or social capital, as a foundation for mutual understanding leading to better outcomes – hopefully, I would wish to add.

Conclusion

The principal–agent framework offers the most general analysis of the problem of hiring someone to work for you with a reimbursement to come from the work effort of this person. Perhaps it offers the only truly general approach to state management, as from it may be deduced a model of bureaucracy (*moral hazard*) as well as a model of contracting out (*adverse selection*). What it reveals most about state management is the strategic aspects of the interaction between government on the one hand and agencies on the other hand: How are teams instructed and motivated to implement governmental intentions? The principal–agent model may engulf the public–private partnerships and state their differences to bureaucracy in a succinct manner.

After all, the delivery of public service fits the principal–agent concept perfectly. Government hires in some ways teams of people to deliver services to the population. These teams would want to get paid for their effort, but how can government observe or verify effort? Opportunism is bound to occur on the part of either government or the agents. Thus, the principal–agent game starts and evolves.

One may also interpret public sector reform as the search for alternative institutions that help resolve aspects of the principal–agent problematic. The principal would want to have public services delivered at reasonable cost and with good quality, but how does one arrive at that basic goal of state management?

One key aspect or question in state management is how decisions are made by the principal, i.e. policies that make the machinery of formal organisation start moving. Policy-making was the answer to the search for new and more informative models of state management. But what, then, is the logic behind the making of public policies and how are they implemented by a variety of agents?

Essential summary

1 The principal–agent perspective upon state management derives from game theory, especially the economics of asymmetric information.
2 Applied to the state, the population would be the ultimate principal of government. But one may also regard the government as the principal of its bureaux, housing the government agents.
3 Principal–agent interaction includes a couple of problematics, such moral hazard or *ex post* opportunism and adverse selection or *ex ante*

opportunism. They may lead to inefficiencies in the supply of public services.

4 According to the principal–agent approach to public services, the crux of the matter involves a few contractual problems. Given the gulf between what is agreed upon *ex ante* and what is accomplished *ex post*, the strategic advantage rests with the agent.

5 A number of strategies may be drawn upon by the principal in order to reduce the information advantage of the agent, including institutional reforms and New Public Management.

Suggested readings

Banks, J. and B. Weingast (1992) "The Political Control of Bureaucracies Under Asymmetric Information", *American Journal of Political Science*, Vol. 36: 509–524.

Gibbons, R. (1998) "Incentives in Organisations", *Journal of Economic Perspectives*, Vol. 12, No. 4: 115–132.

Kreps, D.M. (1990) *A Course in Microeconomic Theory*. New York: Harvester Wheatsheaf.

Laffont, J.-J. and D. Martimort (2001) *The Theory of Incentives: The Principal–Agent Model*. Princeton: Princeton University Press.

Lane, J.-E. (2005) *Public Administration and Public Management: The Principal–Agent Perspective*. London: Routledge.

Leibenstein, H. (1978) *General X-Efficiency Theory and Economic Development*. New York: Oxford University Press.

McCarty, N. and A. Meirowitz (2007) *Political Game Theory: An Introduction*. Cambridge: Cambridge University Press.

McCubbins, M.D., R. Noll and B. Weingast (1989) "Structure and Process, Politics and Policy: Administrative Arrangements and the Political Control of Agencies", *Virginia Law Review*, Vol. 75, March: 431–482. Reprinted in T.P. Lyon (ed.) (2007) *Regulation*. Cheltenham: Edward Elgar.

Moe, T. (2006) "Political Control and the Power of the Agent", *Journal of Law, Economics, and Organisation*, Vol. 22, No. 1: 1–29.

Mueller, D. (2003) *Public Choice III*. Cambridge: Cambridge University Press.

Nurmi, H. (2006) *Models of Political Economy*. London: Routledge.

Rasmusen, E. (2006) *Games and Information: An Introduction to Game Theory*. Oxford: Blackwell.

3 Policy models

How rational is public management?

Introduction

The problem of rationality has always been a core concern in public management. The analysis of public management is both descriptive – what goes on?
– and normative – how can practice be changed? Since public management
involves the handling of huge resources – physical, human, financial and
social, the question of efficiency crops up, time and again. If efficiency may
be improved upon, then how can public organisations be steered towards that
goal in a rational manner?

Public management as policy-making introduced quite a new way of looking at the public sector and its organisations, compared with the formal
organisation approach. It offered a dynamic perspective upon what public
agencies do and how their practice may be changed towards the achievement
of new political goals. Thus, the public sector was reconceptualised into a set
of public policy areas, where the important thing was how policies may be
designed so that they would lead to social improvement.

Public management may be analysed as a means–end chain in order to
underline its rationality requirement. Policies target ultimate goals by the
employment of means at various stages. Thus, one goal is a means to another
goal, etc. In this way, there arises the question of rationality: can ends and
means be identified that satisfy coherence and efficiency? I wish to argue in
favour of a *revised rationality thesis*, stating that the actors participating in
policy-making as well as the implementation of policy may well be behaving
completely rationally, but that the organisation as a whole, government or the
agency, tends to display bounded rationality or sometimes appear foolish.

Policy rationality: the full model

I will begin by stating the complete model of rational state management
first, and after that proceed to examine the theories that question, partially or

completely, that state management could be rational. The concept of rationality refers basically to action, and has been fully developed within economics and game theory. It may be applied to single individuals, taking various actions by themselves, or onto organised collective units, such as organisations, firms or public agencies. The problem of rationality in public management boils down to the question of whether public organisations such as the state, the bureaucracy or the agencies can or do engage in rational decision-making when they act as a collective.

Rational decision-making requires that an actor performs four quite demanding mental operations, namely:

1 Possibilities: identifying all the alternative actions, with an emphasis upon "all".
2 Causality: collecting information upon all outcomes that are connected with the alternative actions. This involves knowing the probabilities that the alternative actions lead to, or their outcomes. Probabilities range from 0 to 1.
3 Utility: deciding a ranking order for the outcomes in terms of priorities that may be stated by means of utility numbers between, for instance, -1 and $+1$.
4 Maximising expected value: choosing the alternative action with the highest score of probability $\times$ utility, summed over all the outcomes of the alternative actions.

This model of choice, rational decision-making, has been the basis for the great advances in microeconomics as well as game theory. When its assumptions apply, then the model delivers precise and often unique predictions. The controversy surrounding this model concerns whether or not the four assumptions above apply in situations other than elementary consumer or producer choices in markets, for instance, for organisations.

One may oppose two extreme views on the applicability of rational decision-making: economic imperialism on the one hand and sociological imperialism on the other hand. A good exponent of the first position is Gary Becker in the Chicago School of Economics whereas the second position is to be found in his most fervent critique, Amitai Etzioni.

Now, for public management the crucial issue is not whether organisational man or political man maximises his/her utility, but whether the organisation as such can do that. It is to the question of macro rationality that we will now turn and analyse the variety of models. We will come back to micro rationality when discussing the economic approaches to public management.

Macro rationality: public management as planning

The model of comprehensive planning is the archetype of rational public management. It was quite fashionable for some time during the 1960s and 1970s. And it has still not lost all relevance, although it is no longer considered as useful as it used to be during the heyday of planning in government.

Planning models for the public sector were often inspired by military planning, where goals could be operationalised in concrete measurable outcomes according to alternative scenarios. They worked reasonably well within physical planning, i.e. overall decision-making concerning the use of space and territory. However, planning only had a short period of flourishing in the proper public sector. The chief difficulty was not the problem of the inherent limits of cognitive capacity with men and women, but the organisational context.

When many people participate in a planning process, then the probability is high that goals will not be stable or unambiguous. When the political actors are replaced as their mandates come to an end, so goals will change, affecting the planning process. New goals may mean that all of the planning has to be redone. Also, the agencies will not merely abide by the goals handed down by the politicians. Agencies develop goals of their own that they bring to the planning process.

Planning is closely connected with certain mathematical tools of decision-making, like operations analysis and optimisation. These techniques require that goals and activities be clearly identifiable and measurable. Thus, an algorithm would outline the steps to take in order to maximise an objective. However, if goals change as participants in the planning process come and leave, then planning loses its key feature, namely, stability.

Planning was conceived as technical decision-making, but it tends to become highly political. The planners see things their way, but the responsibility for planning rests with government. Planning discloses a scenario of events for a future that is seen as unchangeable, bypassing other options. When politicians accept a planning algorithm, then they may relinquish their freedom to act as well as their responsibility.

Planning may initiate conflicts between people who wish to have an impact upon the future course of events. The stakeholders of a planning process may be representatives of the entire society, who turn the planning procedure into a process of bargaining and confrontation, each attempting to exercise some pressure upon politicians or planners. The political nature of planning is nowhere more apparent than in city planning, where decisions are taken about the future shape of the community, involving numerous economic and environmental consequences that become issues. City planning may appear as a neutral process of optimising the future by experts, the city planners. In reality, city planning concerns the basic parameters of the political community and its future forms of life.

During the heyday of planning, it was believed that almost all activities in the public sector would benefit from being modelled in terms of algorithms. Thus, not only would military defence and territorial planning be planned, but also health care and education. One year planning would be linked with five year planning. The planned society would replace the spontaneous or anarchical society. The search for the planned society offset a reaction that resulted in a fundamental critique of planning. Two alternative decision-making models were devised as being more accurately representative of the public sector than the comprehensive rational model. They model public sector decision-making as deviating more or less from the four assumptions cited earlier.

Bounded rationality

Herbert Simon underlined the actual cognitive limitations of human beings when elaborating his model of satisfying decision-making. The four assumptions of the rational model are never fulfilled, because decision-makers do not know all the alternatives of action as well as all the probabilities of outcomes. Thus, they cannot calculate the expected values for all the alternatives.

Faced with these cognitive constraints, human beings develop a more modest decision-making model that focusses upon certain alternatives and takes into account some outcomes. Instead of maximising objectives, men and women satisfy some reasonable targets that are within the limits of human cognitive capacity – the principle of *satisficing*.

Economics and business administration has debated the pros and cons of the model of bounded rationality ever since Simon presented his *Models of Man* (1957). Economists most often wish to defend the rational model, either as a heuristic device or as in agreement with basic notions in game theory such as Bayesian decision-making, whereas scholars in business administration have tended to endorse the model of bounded rationality. A key text supporting Simon was the Cyert and March book *A Behavioral Theory of the Firm* (1963). Another influential economist, Oliver Williamson, also fully endorsed bounded rationality as the conceptual foundation for his theory of the firm. Yet, the debate about the pros and cons of bounded rationality still rages on in economics and business administration. Things were somewhat different with regard to the public sector.

Here bounded rationality scored an almost immediate success. Not only did scholars from organisation theory or the sociology of organisations endorse bounded rationality when approaching organisations in the public sector, but political scientists also found the bounded rationality model much more appealing than the rational decision-making model. Two scholars in favour of accepting the model of bounded rationality were very influential: Charles Lindblom and Aaron Wildavsky.

"Muddling through"

The idea of suboptimalisation in organisations appealed much to analysts of government and bureaucracy. It seemed to account for many of the dysfunctions in the public sector: red tape, redundancies, over or undershooting, inefficiencies, weak productivity, etc. If public sector delivery of services was constrained by cognitive limitations that could not be undone, then perhaps the best strategy was merely to try to muddle through.

Lindblom's articles and books covered the entire policy process, from political decisions to administrative ones. They underlined the impossibility of rational decision-making, recommending that policy-makers try to satisfy, not maximise. Public policy-making was modelled as a protracted process where the final results could not be foreseen at the start. The notion of "muddling through" agreed with sceptical images of government as business as usual, bureaucratic inertia and a Kafkaesque perspective upon the state.

Incrementalism

Wildavsky added intellectual power to concepts of bounded rationality by transforming the model into specific and testable equations (Wildavsky, 1964). It was such a prominent feature of the state as the budget that Wildavsky and associates managed to model in terms of incremental decision-making, adhering basically to bounded rationality. If policies were transformed into budgets at the end of the day, then the policy process should reveal its essential characteristics in the yearly budget-making process. How could government work, after all, without funding? And surely the people who pay also call the tune?

From the perspective of the budget, policy-making could be decomposed into two elements, the base and the increment. While the base, comprising about 80 per cent of the budget, tends to be unchanged in the short-run, the increment or the yearly changes would tend to be volatile, either positively or negatively. Empirical testing of these equations for budgetary requests and budgetary appropriations confirmed incrementalism, at least partially. Thus, the base tended to remain intact and the yearly changes displayed considerable growth stability. Policy-making was indeed bounded rationality (Wildavsky, 1971).

Later, when the seminal process of public sector expansion had come to a halt in the 1980s, the empirical evidence for incrementalism or marginalism failed to show up. Instead, scholars started to identify so-called shift-points in budgeting, indicating a major policy change. If policies could be terminated completely or reformed in an encompassing way, then perhaps decision-making was not bounded rationality?

Before we return to the idea of rational decision-making, it is interesting to make a small detour into the land of organised foolishness. If public management is policy-making, and policy-making falls short of rationality, then perhaps public management is organised anarchy?

Organised anarchy

Models of irrationality were launched by James March, in collaboration with Johan P. Olsen. When public management runs into the garbage can process of decision-making, then public management becomes a host of pathologies: leadership is luck, solutions look for problems and participation becomes fluid. The question that March never answered was, of course, how often would public management run into this kind of collective foolishness?

Two answers were hinted at. On the one hand, public management as policy pathology was a probability. It could occur but it was not necessary. Thus, interesting examples of garbage can processes were collected and analysed. Especially large-scale public sector reform initiatives seemed to face the risk of a garbage can process. Thus, higher education reforms were analysed comparatively in an effort to find out which were successes and which were failures, and why this was so. On the other hand, it was sometimes suggested that public policy is always more or less pathological which entailed that public management could not possibly be rational. Thus, scholars started to look upon budgets as myths, reforms or the lack of them as culture, etc. The idea of organised anarchy fitted well into the post-modernist drive in the late twentieth century, images replacing nature, subjectivity destabilising objectivity, and interpretation substituting probabilities.

Yet, the idea of public management as foolishness was hardly a highly fertile model. If policy-making is always pathological, then what is to be done? Perhaps privatisation is the only alternative to foolishness, if indeed private firms could avoid the garbage can trap? At the same time as modelling the policy process ran its full course, from rationality to irrationality, new ideas about public management were developed, using the model of rationality.

The important distinction, when understanding the emergence of the public choice models of policy-making, is that between macro (group) and micro (individual) rationality. Bounded rationality and garbage can models questioned the possibility for groups of people to engage in a process of rational decision-making, such as a government or a public agency. One may accept this rejection of macro rationality, but still retain micro rationality, i.e. adhere to models that describe persons in public management as actors who maximise their utility. In fact, when such models of micro rationality in public management were launched by economists, adhering to rational individual decision-making, then they became very popular and influential, politically.

Micro rationality: the public choice models

Bypassing macro rationality entirely, individual rationality was re-established in the public choice models of public management. The public choice school resulted from the application of rational models of *choice* to *public* sector decision-making. In public management, the key individuals maximise their self-interest to the same extent as market participants. Thus, the flavour of public management is set by the budget maximising bureaucrat or the revenue maximising politician (Niskanen, 1971 [2007]; Brennan and Buchanan, 1980 [2006]).

The focus upon selfish interests in public management opened up a debate on the role of incentives in the public sector. Instead of assuming that public employees are driven by an abstract entity like the public interest, public management recognised that different performance had to be paid differently. Incentive schemes had to be introduced into the contracts, about jobs and performance, in the public sector. And the concept of incentive compatibility was to have a lasting impact upon human resource management in the public sector.

Yet, the public choice school is more linked with political economy and conservatism than with public management. The lessons from public choice models, whenever they were supported by empirical evidence, which was not always the case, could well be incorporated into public management. The assumption common to all public choice models about public management, i.e. that narrow self-interests are the dominant motivation, provoked considerable criticism as being too blunt and too simple. Thus, for instance, Dunleavy developed a competing theory about the behaviour of bureaux by modifying the basic assumption somewhat. Instead of assuming that bureaucrats maximise their budgets, which is both risky and tedious, he assumed that public agencies adopt a bureau-shaping strategy, aiming at improving the status of the bureau by doing more intelligence work and providing less concrete services (Dunleavy, 1991).

Individual rationality has also come back in budget studies, partly due to rapid advances in game theory in the second half of the twentieth century. In the well-known Baron and Ferejohn budgetary equations, modelling budgeting in Congress, the four typical assumptions of the rational model are assumed to be correct at the individual level. Explaining budgetary outcomes like expenditure and taxation decisions, it is not necessary to deviate to bounded rationality.

The key problem: is rationality feasible in government?

Economists work with two alternative concepts of rationality. For one, most economists (the majority) adhere to the neo-classical model, assuming full or complete rationality with maximising men and women. However, many of them would only admit that it is a working hypothesis and not a general truth. On the other hand, some (the minority) reject *homo economicus* in order to endorse the model of bounded rationality, or the assumption of incomplete or partial rationality with satisfying men and women. Very few accept the model of men or women as irrational beings. This holds for the micro situation, i.e. how human beings behave singularly. Matters become more difficult when decision-making in organisations or government is to be modelled.

Political scientists and sociologists tend to endorse bounded rationality more than complete rationality, although the rational choice approach is gaining more and more adherents in the two disciplines. One major reason for the adherence to bounded rationality is that it seems more convincing than complete rationality when the macro level is to be modelled: how do organised collectivities decide?

The problem is the step from the micro level to the macro level. As it seems difficult to maintain that governments or organisations as a whole proceed along the rational choice model outlined earlier, one draws the conclusion that bounded rationality is true of state management. However, one must distinguish the micro level from the macro level. One may assume that individuals tend to follow the complete model of rationality, but the outcomes at the macro level may be anything, from complete rationality to organised foolishness.

The most persuasive argument against bounded rationality has come from recent advances in game theory, elaborated by, for example, Harsanyi and Selten. According to the micro foundations of game theory, a player will always use all available information at time t. It may not be complete or perfect, but as soon as he/she finds out that new information is forthcoming he/she will take it into account at time $t + 1$. Thus, incomplete or imperfect information is only temporary. The rational expectations hypothesis in economics offers the same idea, which, it seems, undoes the relevance of bounded rationality.

Beyond rationality in policy-making

Recently, scholars have ventured beyond the problem of rationality in the policy process, introducing other relevant aspects, such as influence, transparency and accountability. It is no longer enough that legislators are very involved in policy-making or that the government is democratically elected. Policy-making should also be open to influence not only from organised interests, attempting to capture the dynamics of the process for their demands, but also to more legitimate stakeholders such as citizen groups and civil society. Multiculturalism also pushes its way into the policy-making process, calling for explicit taking into account of the variety of minorities (Birkland, 2001).

Broadening the policy process to make it accessible to a variety of groups can be done in several ways. Some countries have attempted to formalise widespread participation and input into the policy process, including hearings, consultations, *ad hoc* committees, trade union inclusion, etc.

Assessing policy-making from other aspects of rationality leads to the consideration of other values, such as influence, accountability and transparency. Taking these values into account may result in trade-offs with the efficiency of the policy-making process, as policies may take longer to be enacted and also face considerable risk of being diluted in a slow process.

Conclusion

The question about rationality in public management has been a long standing theme, inviting numerous arguments and counter-arguments. It was the equation of public management with public policy that started this debate, as it was somehow believed that there was something that could be called "rational" policy-making. When one separates between individual rationality and group rationality, then much of the puzzle of rationality in public management disappears. One may wish to allow for the possibility that actors may be rational in the public sector but putting the probability that organised collectivities like governments, bureaucracies and public enterprises can be rational low.

I believe that a modified rationality thesis may be rescued, referring to the micro level. It seems that game theory and the rational expectations revolution in economics has vindicated the relevance of the rational choice approach (Gibbons, 1992; Rotheli, 2007). But whereas actors may be modelled as pursuing their preferences rationally, no one has shown that aggregates such as governments or bureaux may achieve full rationality.

The emergence of the policy paradigm was a reply to the question that the formal organisation approach logically raised: what do bureaucracies do when they follow, more or less, their rules? Reply: They deliver public services in accordance with some objectives. A policy is a means–end chain that links the activities of an agency with political goals. Thus, every domain of the public sector has, at least in principle, a policy, and public management is policy-making. Yet, it was soon discovered that something had been left out, the so-called missing link.

The principal–agent approach may be applied to all that takes place in the public sector, once policies have been enacted. Analytically speaking, state management starts with policy-making in government and the representative assembly, resulting in a huge set of programmes, supported by budgets and laws/regulations. It is empirically true that the policy cycle is a circular one, as implementation affects policy and vice versa (May and Wildavsky, 1979). Yet, after any enactment of policy, government needs to hire agents to do the work, whatever it might be. Principal–agent interaction or gaming surfaces in all the mechanisms are designed to put policy into effect such as, for instance:

- bureaucracy
- regulatory agencies
- policy networks
- incorporated public firms
- outsourcing to private agents
- financial bailouts
- pension or unemployment funds.

Government cannot operate a variety of public programmes without sets of employees – teams. They possess an asymmetric information advantage for which they wish to receive a rent of some sort. The art of state management is to handle the incentive problematic in motivating teams to carry out public programmes as effectively as possible, given the restrictions that emanate from moral hazard and adverse selection. Thus, state management basically presents a vast set of contractual difficulties, to be resolved on the basis of the respect for rule of law. Public policies will be put into practice through a nexus of contracts between principals and agents.

Essential summary

1 Questions about the rationality of public policies may be divided into micro and macro rationality. Thus, one may ask whether the individual policy-makers act according to the rational decision-making model, as well as whether aggregates such as a government, a bureau or the state take decisions according to the rational decision-making model.

2 Policy-making is often incremental, meaning that the policy-makers apply the bounded rationality model, especially when making budgets.

3 Policy-making occasionally runs into a garbage can process, meaning that policies become foolish and impossible to implement successfully.

4   The rational decision-making model is clearly relevant when explaining the micro motives of individual policy-makers, but it is not so illuminating when it comes to the choice behaviour of groups, like the government, the legislature or the courts and tribunals.
5   The relevance of micro rationality for modelling single actors comes out well in game theory, especially in Bayesian updating.

Suggested readings

Baron, D.P. and J.A. Ferejohn (1989) "Bargaining in Legislatures", *American Political Science Review*, Vol. LXXXIII, 1181–1206.

Becker, G.S. (1995) *The Essence of Becker*. Stanford: Hoover Institution Press.

Birkland, T.A. (2001) *An Introduction to the Policy Process: Theories, Concepts and Models of Public Policy Making*. Armonk, NY: M.E. Sharpe.

Brennan, G. and J.M. Buchanan (1980, 2006) *The Power to Tax: Analytic Foundations of a Fiscal Constitution*. Cambridge: Cambridge University Press.

Cyert, R. and J. March (1992) *Behavioral Theory of the Firm*. Oxford: Blackwell.

Dunleavy, P. (1991) *Bureaucracy and Public Choice: Economic Explanations in Political Science*. New York: Longman.

Etzioni, A. (1990) *The Moral Dimension*. New York: Free Press.

Gibbons, R. (1992) *A Primer in Game Theory*. London: Harvester Wheatsheaf.

March, J. (1989) *Decision and Organisations*. Oxford: Blackwell.

March, J.G. and J.P. Olsen (1976) *Ambiguity and Choice in Organizations*. Oslo: Universitetsforlaget.

May, J.V. and A. Wildavsky (eds) (1979) *The Policy Cycle*. Beverley Hills, CA: Sage.

Moran, M., M. Rein and R.E. Goodin (eds) (2006) *The Oxford Handbook of Public Policy*. Oxford: Oxford University Press.

Niskanen, W.A. (1971, 2007) *Bureaucracy and Representative Government*. Edison, NJ: Transaction Publishers.

Rotheli, T.F. (2007) *Expectations, Rationality and Economic Performance: Models and Experiments*. Cheltenham: Edward Elgar.

Simon, H.A. (1997) *Administrative Behavior: A Study of Decision-Making Processes in Administrative Organisations.* New York: Simon & Schuster.

Wildavsky, A. (2006) *Budgeting and Governing*, with B. Swedlow (ed.) and J. White (Introduction). Edison, NJ: Transaction Publishers.

—— (1971) *The Revolt Against the Masses and Other Essays on Politics and Public Policy*. Edison, NJ: Transaction Publishers.

—— (1964) *The Politics of the Budgetary Process*. Boston: Little Brown. See also *The New Politics of the Budgetary Process* by A. Wildavsky and N. Caiden (2003), New York: Longman.

4 Implementation models

Bringing outcomes into public management and policy

Introduction

State management could not merely be planning or policy-making. It must also include outcomes or results. Once one starts looking upon the public sector as policy outputs, then one is forced to also examine policy outcomes. And the gulf between intended outcomes and real outcomes is a main warning against any attempt to model public management as rational from the point of view of government or the agency.

The link between policy and outcomes was called "implementation" and it was named the missing link in the study of public management. Implementation analysis surfaced in the 1980s as a new approach to public management, where the key problem was how to identify successful implementation and distinguish it from implementation failure.

If public management is implementation, then the centre of attention must be shifted from policy-making to policy implementation. This in turn requires that outcomes be scrutinised: intended and unintended, recognised and unrecognised, successful and unsuccessful. If public management involves a big dose of outcomes, then what is the link between service delivery and outcomes?

The problem of implementation

Pressman and Wildavsky stated the problem of implementation in their 1973 book: policies do not translate automatically into a set of well-defined outcomes that accomplish the policy objectives. Instead, policies tend to be difficult to implement, i.e. put into practice in a successful manner. This objection by Pressman and Wildavsky (1973, 1984) may be raised against any naïve policy theory, as it can actually be launched against all forms of public administration including law, focussing upon decisions and documents high up in the hierarchy. The realisation of this gulf between policy and outcome added a whole new dimension to public management, namely, the effort to understand results better (Hjern and Porter, 1981).

The implementation perspective upon public management made it vulnerable to the criticism that outcomes did not match up to promises. Various forms of outcome analyses were added to policy analysis, such as social indicator assessment, social impact analysis, urban outcomes, quality of life indices, etc. The impact of the implementation approach upon public management was so large that centres and institutes were set up to handle the vast need for information about results.

Public management as implementation goes far beyond public management as bureaucracy or formal organisation. It is not enough to run a set of operations, more or less efficiently, as what matters most is the achievement of objectives. Nor it is enough to focus upon policy objectives, as results may be far away from them. Public management as implementation implies that it is vital to figure out what is really going on within huge bureaucracies, as well as pin down what the impact of public services upon society is.

If public management cannot be done without a profound understanding of outcomes and their analysis, then public management would also have to include a theory about how good outcomes can be promoted. Thus, there arises the question of the best implementation strategy.

The concept of implementation gap meant a lethal blow to the central planning approach. If public management has an endemic split between policy-making in its representative institutions and at the central government level on the one hand and the actual putting in practice of programmes at lower levels of government, then the theory of public management must acknowledge this and build models that take this hiatus into account.

Implementation models

Once public management understands the hiatus between goals and results, one can start reflecting upon how to diminish this gap. In the implementation approach to public management, there was, from the outset, a strong scepticism about top-down implementation. Actually, hierarchy was blamed for the mismatch between intentions and results. Thus, the search early on was for models of implementation that would reduce the hiatus.

Top-down implementation was identified as political centralisation with a preference for bureaucracy. It was also linked with planning, and thus dismissed due to the scepticism surrounding central planning frameworks. Public management as implementation was first and foremost a realisation that the lower echelons in the state may be as important as the higher echelons. The implementation perspective favoured the so-called street-level bureaucrats in the public sector, i.e. public employees like nurses, teachers and policemen.

What emerged from the search for ways to narrow the hiatus was the bottom-up model of implementation (Hjern and Porter, 1981). It presented a strong anti-dose against top-down perspectives and could easily be integrated into new theories about public management underlining learning and flexibility (Pressman and Wildavsky, 1984). If putting policies into practice was difficult and higher level planning was bound to fail, then why not trust lower levels in the hierarchy of the state with the full responsibility of enforcing policies? At least there could not be another more effective model of implementation.

Whereas formal organisation involves a static perspective upon public management, policy implementation is inherently dynamic in its viewpoint. Models of implementation would outline how public management should go about things when putting policies into practice. Several implementation studies examined how big public sector reforms were enacted and what the outcomes were. But it required little imagination to take the step towards the concept of implementation as an ongoing concern. Implementation and public management became inseparable, as both dealt with the ongoing effort to improve public services and their outcomes.

Politics as nested games

Public management as implementation ended all forms of naïvety about public services and their delivery. Gone was the effort to pretend that an abstract organisational scheme could capture the essential elements in public service delivery. Gone also was the presumption that national unified schemes for service delivery could be constructed at the top of government. The implementation perspective destroyed the alleged advantages of hierarchy.

Fritz Scharpf formulated a model that captured this scepticism about formal organisation and hierarchy – *politikverflechtung*. It was basically a model about joint decision-making and implementation in Germany, but it could be generalised to any state framework. It is also relevant to regional bodies and the new theme of so-called multi-level government.

"Joint decision-making" involves the hierarchical subordination between the central government and the regional or local governments being replaced by a system of co-decision-making, independent implementation and mutual veto. Thus, German federalism deviates from the classical model of dualistic federalism with a clear separation between the federal government and the states. In Germany, the states participate very much in the federal government through their direct participation in the federal chamber, deciding about framework legislation as well as taxes and grants. In addition, implementation of federal laws is a task for the *Länder*. According to Scharpf, this leads to a conflation of political authority onto many players who can obstruct each other, thereby delaying necessary policy changes – *the joint decision trap*.

The question that the *theme of politics nesting* raises is whether it applies more or less to all political systems with three-tier levels of government. Scharpf suggested that the construction of the EU led to this joint decision trap. What is similar between the Federal Republic of Germany and the European Union is that various levels of government are nested in a complex web of decision-making and implementation. Only the European Court of Justice (ECJ) has a clear authority-command structure, being the sovereign legal body of the union. Yet, in dualistic federal systems, as well as in decentralised unitary systems, the nesting of politics and administration may be avoided to some extent by clear lines of subordination on the one hand and autonomy on the other hand.

Institutional design tends to be preoccupied with separating functions and levels in the state. Thus, for instance, dualistic federalism attempts to come up with a comprehensive and exhaustive list of competences, to be allocated in a consistent and clear way. Also, unitary states try to fix the functions and competences for lower levels of government such as communes and county councils. However, realities deny all such clear-cut distinctions, according to the model of *politikverflechtung*.

When policies are transformed into activities and activities give rise to outcomes, then various decision-making bodies at different kinds of levels of government become interwoven, nested or interlocked. Thus, there is no real centre of governance, only mutual interdependencies. Add the regional dimension in, for instance, the form of the European Union, and these interconnections result in networks that can only be productive if they score high on coordination, i.e. consensus.

Implementation as coalitions

When public management is equated with implementation, then it is not necessary to stay within the confines of the state. Thus, Sabatier and Jenkins-Smith suggested that implementation is often driven by so-called advocacy coalitions, consisting of various actors, including different government agencies, associations, civil society organisations, think tanks, academics, media institutions, and prominent individuals. The advocacy coalition framework modelled the importance of various coalitions between certain policy-makers, influential actors and pressure groups. Such coalitions would form on the basis of shared beliefs and values, as actors/organisations sharing a similar perspective forge relationships with each other.

Public management conceived as coalition building highlights the dynamic perspective upon policy-making. Such coalitions may be temporary, as when one comprehensive reform is to be made. Or they may be in continuous operation, as with policy networks. According to Sabatier and Jenkins-Smith, there may be competing advocacy coalitions within each policy domain. One of these coalitions would then be dominant, with more power over the policy process than other coalitions. Academics and think tanks have a far greater chance of being heard when there are like-minded influential politicians in the dominant advocacy coalition. Advocacy coalitions would not usually give up their core values and beliefs. But as they are open to changes of 'secondary importance' such as specific policy formulations, academic research has a role to play in assisting them. Thus, academic research may help such coalitions producing better arguments, sometimes in relation to the claims of their opponents.

Policy implementation conceived as learning (Pressman and Wildavsky, 1984) or coalition formation (Sabatier and Jenkins-Smith, 1993) fits much better with the bottom-up approach to implementation than with the top-down approach. It focuses upon things entirely different from formal organisation and it is inherently dynamic in outlook.

Implementation analysis often examined big one-shot reforms of the public sector such as the introduction of new higher education institutions, or the decentralisation of the state. And it aimed at discovering the necessary and sufficient conditions for successful implementation of such huge reforms. However, there is nothing that excludes implementation analysis from dealing with the ongoing execution of minor policies over a longer time span. Public management then becomes the governance of coalitions, i.e. policy networks linking up the stakeholders of public programmes including private actors or interests.

The key problem: could implementation be made self-fulfilling?

With so much interest focussed upon the implementation gap, it is small wonder that one has searched for a mechanism that could facilitate successful implementation. If control by higher level bureaucrats of lower level ones is not the answer, then how can lower level bureaucrats become interested in promoting good outputs and outcomes? One answer was fixers, i.e. certain persons who tend to emerge in organisations and become the trouble shooters. Another answer was the advocacy coalition approach that directly and explicitly included the stakeholders in the implementation process. Finally, there is the answer from network theory, i.e. build a public–private partnership.

The resolution of the implementation gap probably lies in handling incentives, so that lower level bureaucrats develop a stake in successful outcomes. If reinventing government was an effort to do exactly that, then it was a step in the right direction. However, as long as it is impossible to directly link the remuneration of a bureaucrat with the value that he/she generates, incentives schemes will not be strategy proof against all forms of opportunism. Implementation is a matter for contracting, i.e. how to write and enforce an agreement with the implementers of policy that they deliver high quality services at low cost. The theory of bureaucracy offered one contract – long-term, or tenure, while NPM offers a completely different one – short-term.

Whether the implementation process will result in successful implementation all depends upon two key parameters: information and incentives. Promoting good outcomes or the results that government wants, the people responsible for implementation will need not only relevant information, but will also need to be highly motivated. Top-down implementation suffers from a lack of local acquaintance and incapacity to mobilise local support and enthusiasm. Bottom-up implementation may lead to too much local variety, including attention to local idiosyncrasies. A decentralised approach to information gathering (learning) and the mobilisation of motivation is favoured in the network framework.

If one answers the question posed earlier positively, then one adheres to the bottom-up approach to implementation, searching for groups of people who have incentives of their own to bring policies into effect. In the prolongation of the bottom-up approach one encounters new ideas about self-implementing organisations, such as the network model that has attracted much attention in both public management and public administration.

If one, on the contrary, replies negatively to the above question, then one adheres to the top-down approach. A recent, new version of this framework is the policy instruments model. Inspired by economic policy theory, some scholars have developed a theory of policy instruments as tools of government. The idea is that each policy – environmental, education, health care – would have a limited set of instruments to be employed in implementation. Analysing a set of policy instruments, one is interested in aspects like the coherence or conflicts of instruments, their degree of substitutability and their comparative efficacy. Yet, a lesson from the study of policy instruments is distinctly bottom-up, namely, that the use of policy instrument is dependent upon the social context and the institutional set-up. Besides, there is constant learning about these policy instruments and their innovation (Eliadis *et al.*, 2005; Salamon, 2002).

Implementation is never automatic

The main lesson from the studies of policy implementation is that implementation can never be taken for granted. To implement a policy successfully requires a lot of effort on the part of many people and it calls for the elaboration of a strategy concerning how to go about putting a policy into practice.

The search for a theory of implementation as a self-adjusting or self-correcting mechanism, i.e. an automatic process of learning and correction, has not materialised. Instead, scholars have offered a bundle of theories of implementation that, however different they may be, underline that perfect implementation is never certain or highly probable. The following chapters will examine the pros and cons of these alternative implementation mechanisms: agencification, networks, internal markets, contracting in and contracting out, and incorporation.

Conclusion

The idea of the implementation gap redirected the entire field of public management away from a close reading of legislation and budgetary appropriations towards theorising what actually goes on beneath the parliament and the central agencies. It underlined the criticism of the formal organisation framework by stating the relevance of informal mechanisms, such as the "fixers" in implementation or the "advocacy coalitions" driving change processes.

The implementation focus opened up public management to the recognition of the fundamental importance of the concept of an outcome for public sector governance. What mattered most at the end of the day was, of course, whether the delivery of public services really worked, as measured by key outcome performance scores. The implementation perspective led to the discovery of the relevance of outcomes to public management by insisting upon the implementation gap, i.e. the systematic difference between central government goals in public sector reforms and the actual putting in practice of programmes funded by these same reforms. The missing link between high profile objectives and concrete practices is *implementation steering* or, as one would call it today, public management.

I suggest the thesis that *implementation is open-ended*, meaning that there is no approach or policy instrument that can guarantee successful implementation. The problem of implementation recurs when state management is modelled as agencification or incorporation as well as policy networks and NPM. In reality, the question of successful implementation mars the delivery of public services. The only certain thing is that successful implementation is more probable when there is a mix of incentives and contracts that enhance efficient outputs and outcomes – what game theorists call *incentive compatibility*.

Essential summary

1 "Implementation" refers to the entire process of putting a policy into practice, covering both so-called policy outputs and policy outcomes.

2   The implementation gap stands for the often large distance between the intention behind a policy (goals and means) and what has been achieved in reality – the outcomes.

3   An implementation strategy is a deliberate design of a mechanism that may help close this gap.

4   Two implementation strategies have been much debated: top-down implementation and bottom-up implementation. And their pros and cons are evaluated differently in implementation research.

5   Implementation may be a one-shot game, as with introducing a new major policy innovation, or implementation is continuous, an ongoing endeavour.

6   Implementation research at first underlined hierarchy, but more recent implementation studies emphasise the bottom-up approach with learning, advocacy coalitions and networks.

7   In vain, implementation research has looked for a self-implementing mechanism or an organisation that would be self-adjusting to external stimuli that affect successful policy implementation.

Suggested readings

Eliadis, P., M.M. Hill, and M. Howlett (eds) (2005) *Designing Government: From Instruments to Governance*, Montreal: McGill-Queen's University Press.

Hill, M. (ed.) (1997) *The Policy Process: A Reader*. New York: Prentice Hall.

Hjern, B. and M. Porter (1981) "Implementation Structures: A New Unit of Analysis", *Organization Studies*, Vol. 2, No. 3: 211–227.

Lipsky, M. (1983) *Street-Level Bureaucracy: Dilemmas of the Individual in Public Service*. New York: Russell Sage Foundation.

Marsh, D., D. Richards and M.J. Smith (2001) *Changing Patterns of Governance in the United Kingdom: Reinventing Whitehall?* Basingstoke: Palgrave Macmillan.

Pressman, J. and A. Wildavsky (1973, 1984) *Implementation*. Berkeley: University of California Press.

Sabatier, P.A. (ed.) (2006) *Theories of the Policy Process*. Boulder, CO: Westview Press.

Sabatier, P.A. and H.C. Jenkins-Smith (eds) (1993) *Policy Change and Learning: Advocacy Coalition Approach*. Boulder, CO: Westview Press.

Salamon, L.M. (ed.) (2002) *The Tools of Government: A Guide to the New Governance*. Oxford: Oxford University Press.

Scharpf, F.W. (1997) *Games Real Actors Play: Actor-Centered Institutionalism in Policy Research*. Boulder, CO: Westview Press.

5 Independent agencies
Maximising efficiency?

Introduction

Public management as *agencification* has figured prominently in the public sector reforms in many countries, as governments have searched for organisational alternatives to the traditional departmental structure. The emphasis when setting up and funding agencies is on getting things done while being able to predict the costs of running the new agency. Government should be at arm's length, only monitoring the main results and never interfering in the conduct of daily operations. That is a task for top- and middle-level managers. Thus, the performance of semi-independent bodies may be more easily monitored than in-house activities in a huge government ministry.

Yet, it may be very difficult to pin down the legal nature of the various agencies created recently, whether public or semi-public, autonomous or semi-autonomous (Wettenhall, 2005). To get the job done, government has engaged in a large-scale institutional innovation, relying more than before upon agencies created in an *ad hoc* manner. The general concept for this trend is *unbundled government*, which may occur at both central, regional and local levels of government. It is a trend that fits well with the emphasis on outputs and outcomes as well as cost efficiency. No country has unbundled its state to such an extent as Great Britain.

The British experience: quangos, NDPBs and executive agencies

The term "quango" stems from British public sector reforms. It enters as one of the strategies in the sweeping change within the British state since Thatcher came to power. British public sector reforms have undone the monolithic character of the bureaucracy in the UK, transforming or unbundling the state into various elements: departments, agencies, boards, incorporations, etc. The development of the terminology of quangos is telling.

The words "qango" and "quango", meaning quasi non-governmental organisation, have been used in the UK, Australia and Ireland to denote organisations of various types to which governments have devolved power. The UK government's definition of a non-departmental public body or quango in 1997 was: "A body which has a role in the processes of national government, but is not a government department or part of one, and which accordingly operates to a greater or lesser extent at arm's length from Ministers" (http://en.wikipedia.org/wiki/QUANGO).

The word "quango" referred to a non-governmental organisation that performed governmental functions with government funding or other public support. One example mentioned for Australia was the Red Cross, providing blood bank services, with government support and backing of various kinds. The examples referred to in the UK included bodies like the Press Council and the Law Society, i.e. private bodies engaging in regulation. The use of quangos in the UK led to a fierce debate about the desirability of such non-governmental or quasi-governmental authorities (Flinders and Smith, 1998), not without similarities to experiences in other countries (Greve *et al.*, 1999).

The word "quango" has largely been abandoned in UK official usage for the less controversial term non-departmental public body – the NDPB. It is now used to describe many of the organisations with devolved governmental roles. The use of executive agencies with service delivery functions has developed alongside NDPBs in the UK. These agencies do not usually have a legal identity separate from that of their parent department. When they have trading fund status, then their accounts do not form part of the accounts of the parent department.

In the National Health Service, bodies called "Special Health Authorities" have evolved, which are technically neither NDPBs nor executive agencies. The Department of Health collectively describes all three types as "arm's length bodies" and their creation on a massive scale has been typical of public sector reform in the UK – the splitting apart of the public sector.

Executive agencies

The so-called Next Steps Initiative attracted much attention, because the core of the British state – Whitehall – became the target of cutting up huge departments into a set of small and neat agencies. An executive agency is a part of a government department, but it is treated as managerially and budgetarily separate in order for it to carry out some part-executive functions. The use of executive agencies has been driven by the ambition to distance ministers and the policy divisions of their departments from responsibility for day-to-day policy delivery. Yet, there are legally important differences between these "machinery of government" devices and non-ministerial government departments on the one hand, and non-departmental public bodies ("quangos") on the other, when the latter enjoy constitutional separation from ministerial control.

Typical of agencification is that the earlier hierarchy of command among civil servants is replaced by bargaining between department and agency. First, executive agencies are units reliant on their ministers for their powers to act and contract. Thus, they have no legal status of their own. Yet, the aim is that of separation, of guided autonomy and direct accountability. Second, the government departments are required to exercise close control over an agency's business via budgetary controls, service level agreements, business plans, etc. The staff of executive agencies include civil servants. Each department maintains a "sponsor unit" to oversee, bargain with and monitor each of its agencies.

The Fraser Report of 1991 examined what outcomes had emerged from the new model of an executive agency. It recommended that further powers be devolved from ministers to chief executives. As of July 2002, there were 127 executive agencies, of which 92 report to departments within UK central government, while the remaining 35 belong under the Scottish Executive, Welsh Assembly or Northern Ireland Executive. According to Gains (2003: 56), we have "currently .... 127 executive agencies with approximately 80 percent of civil servants working in agencies or departments run on agency lines".

It has been shown that the executive agency model slowly became the standard model for delivering public services in the United Kingdom. By 1997, 76 per cent of civil servants were employed by an agency. The new Labour government in the *1998 Next Steps Report* endorsed the model in principle. One review in 2002 had two conclusions, one being that the agency model has been a success. Since 1988 agencies have transformed the landscape of government and the responsiveness and effectiveness of services delivered by government. However, it also pointed out that some agencies had become disconnected from their departments. The gulf between policy and delivery is considered by most to have widened. Thus, the evaluation of the British executive agencies has resulted in an ambiguous verdict with contradictory positions, to say the least (James, 2004; Pollitt *et al.*, 2004; Talbot, 2004). The key question may be stated in terms of the principal–agent model: does the creation of an executive agency allow the government as principal to better control the output of its teams or employees than within a traditional departmental structure?

Agencification in other countries

Resorting to a variety of agencies for service delivery and regulatory tasks is not unique to the British government or even the Anglo-Saxon public sector reforms. Continental European countries have also shown an interest in finding new organisational forms that may improve on public sector performance. However, the legalistic spirit that is so dominant in the continental *Rechtsstaat* makes central government a less likely site for agencification, and local government a more likely site for agencification.

The variety of forms for these agencies or bodies is so large that one may ask what their common core is. They do not need legislative approval, as they need not be statutory agencies. And they can be public–private partnerships, meaning that they are not always entirely public bodies.

Agencification counteracts the monolithic public sector, as outlined in the formal organisation approach. Agencies are introduced *ad hoc* and for a limited period of time. They are supposed to deliver and be held accountable for that when the question of their renewal comes up. They may be funded by a government grant or may have some capacity to generate their own revenues. They may deliver services or be responsible for contracting with other service delivery agents.

"Camping on seesaws"

Public management as agencification has left several scholars in a state of confusion, asking what the basic forms of public organisation are. The unbundling of government has gone so far that one may expect almost any kind of organisational form as qualified to be a public agency. In addition, there are all kinds of public–private partnerships as well as the frequent employment of the incorporated organisation in the public sector. Agencification is caused by the dislike of organisational inertia.

The search for new forms of organisation in public sector reform tends to be driven by considerations of expediency, although legal tradition also plays a role. The concept of an executive agency is very much framed on the basis of efficiency considerations, meaning that they are highly output orientated, have a short-term existence, possess clear lines of accountability and are flexible in termination or transformation. The legal traditions of a country restrain organisational innovation by demanding that public bodies have a certain shape, but they do not make new public organisation impossible. Besides, law also changes, as new institutions become accepted and embedded in new legal thought.

Agencification aims to find the least costly and most effective form of organising the provision of a public service. It does not want to use the traditional structure of a department or a statutory body, since they tend to acquire organisational inertia. Public organisations have an inbuilt tendency towards immortality (Kaufman, 1991). To counteract this drive, agencification employs highly flexible and malleable forms of public bodies. Executive agencies are not to be controlled by parliament, but are to serve the best interests of government in delivering services without attempting to erect castles. Agencification in the state corresponds to the drive for "Camping on Seesaws" in management theory (Hedberg *et al.*, 1976). Anything goes in terms of form, as long as the organisation delivers.

The ambition to reduce organisational inertia comes, however, with the cost of neglecting questions of accountability and legitimacy. To some, the trade-off between efficiency and accountability is acceptable, whereas to others it is not. Rule of law considerations do not come high in priority in agencification. But there is a more serious objection to agencification, meaning that it raises a question about the goal of effectiveness itself.

There are many different forms of public organisation, for instance, ministries, departments, authorities, boards, agencies (constitutional, statutory and executive), public companies, trading departments, trusts and associations (Thynne, 2003). This organisational diversity reflects both alternative legal requirements and flexibility in setting up organisations for particular services. When this organisational diversity is combined with public–private partnerships, then the modern public sector presents a jungle of alternative institutions.

The key problem: can policy be separated from delivery?

In the effort to get things done, agencification focusses exclusively on outputs and outcomes. In a big department, the various functions are to be separated out and an *ad hoc* organisation created in order to focus all the attention of the employees upon the delivery of a set of services at the least expensive cost structure possible. When the functions change, then the organisation may be transformed into a new one.

Yet, public organisations do not only deliver services. They also help in making policy. Policy-making is essential to the public sector and its myriad programmes, as it offers evaluation of what is done and suggests improvements or innovations. By separating delivery and policy-making, government may receive less relevant information, not being in touch with what really goes on.

Public management as agencification faces a trade-off between short-term gains in increased focus upon concrete service deliveries against long-term policy relevance of these services. Things change, not only in the market place but also in the public sector. Thus, technology in service delivery develops rapidly and new services may be called for. How can an executive agency respond to these strategic challenges, when it is exclusively oriented towards the daily delivery of services?

Agencification may reduce the overall control of government over the various public sectors, not enhancing its capacity to respond to new demands with policy innovation. It may also make it more difficult for ministries to get correct information about what services are actually delivered and how, as executive agencies pursue their own organisational interests (Hood *et al.*, 2005).

A variety of agencies but the same problem

Countries have different institutional practices in distinguishing between various agencies: ministerial departments, local or regional authorities, commissions or boards and other organisations. The third category is made up of a governmental administrative body that has its own statutory powers and responsibilities. Countries have different practices in designing their central government apparatus, some emphasising big ministerial departments and others employing a set of statutory agencies outside of the ministries that would then tend to be rather small. Countries also differ when it comes to designing the semi-independent agencies, commissions and boards as well as funding them, blurring the distinction between them and the fringe organisations that sometimes evolve in the public sector or on its border lines ("quangos"). Finally, countries make the separation between agencies doing business and agencies merely engaging in administration or regulation in various ways, some relying upon public law and others using private law concepts.

To merely indicate the variety of agencies, I will refer briefly to UK praxis (http://www.nuffield.ox.ac.uk/Politics/Whitehall/Machinery.html), where matters used to be rather clear. Here, agencies outside of ministries include: "non-departmental organisation, non-departmental agency, public body, interstitial organisation, *ad hoc* agency, statutory authority, paragovernmental agency, parastatal agency, fringe body and intermediate body". A classical taxonomy employed the following distinctions: "managerial-economic", "managerial-social" and "regulatory-social" agencies. Thus, we would have the following activities of agencies: (1) commercial operations running an industry or public utility according to commercial principles; (2) social service corporations offering particular social service on behalf of the government; (3) supervisory public corporations with mostly administrative and supervisory functions (Hogwood, 1995: 208).

Another classic UK typology focusses on how the agency is related to government: (1) set up by Act of Parliament; (2) financed by grants-in-aid; (3) chairman appointed by a minister; (4) staff are non-civil servants, recruited and employed by the board or council of a fringe body; (5) annual accounts submitted to the sponsoring minister and laid before Parliament; and (6) annual report published. Yet, after the NPM revolution in the UK, agencies are less neatly classified.

Thus, the classification of so-called fringe bodies in the UK would include executive bodies, advisory bodies, special tribunals, certain public corporations and a variety of health care bodies. Here one would also find advisory bodies set up by administrative action, as well as royal commissions or commissions of inquiry. Given that outsourcing is regularly employed in the UK, it remains ambiguous how some of the agencies are to be classified, for instance, when private agencies, not necessarily located even in the UK, perform public tasks.

The legal position of an agency varies in proportion to the imaginative use of public law distinctions. Almost anything goes, as long as there is some authorisation of some sort to the agency. Yet, underneath the immense variety in agency forms, there is one and the same problem: the accountability of the agency to government. Agencies may be accountable to the executive arm of government or the legislative arm. But their rationale is to deliver services in relation to their mission, given an efficiency restriction. In game theory, this relationship of accountability between government and its agencies is analysed from the principal–agent approach.

Conclusion

Public management as agencification has increased organisational heterogeneity in the state. The adherents argue that organisational innovation is like camping on seesaws, finding whatever works best momentarily in terms of effective service delivery, changing whenever necessary or possible after a couple of years. The detractors look upon organisational multiplicity as a threat to rule of law at worst, and at best, slightly helpful in integrating policy and delivery. Agencification promotes malleability in government, reducing the traditional organisational inertia of bureaucracy.

Yet, agencification definitely rests upon a crude notion of managerialism, taken over from the private sector. If public sector services could be completely identified and measured, then one could set up an organisation solely for the purpose of allocation of these services. However, if all public services are not so easily delineated and if they evolve over time in response to social change, then agencification may only deliver short-term gains. The units within a ministry are not merely production teams, but they also provide information that is valuable in a long-term policy perspective. If fungible and, later on, sold out, they may hollow out the state, depriving it of asset-specific human capital.

One may question whether agencification promotes the generation of trust in the post-bureaucratic public organisation. I believe that the idea of an executive agency belongs more to the philosophy of managerialism than to the idea of the relevance of social capital in public organisations. Yet, the amount of interest focussed upon agencification serves to underscore the relevance of the principal–agent perspective upon state management. It matters how agents are set up in organisations and defined in terms of legal schemes.

Essential summary

1   Much of the work in state management is accomplished by means of agencies, comprising a variety of public employees. But what is an agency?
2   A variety of agencies may be identified in different taxonomies. It matters whether they are statutory agencies or not, whether they are trading department or not, whether they can levy charges or not. Some agencies are oriented towards the production of goods or services, whereas other agencies may be intelligence bureaux or regulatory boards.
3   Most public agencies belong under a government, central, regional or local. But parliament may operate a number of agencies, some of which make inquiries into the governmental ones.
4   A central theme is agency autonomy, or the idea that agencies at arm's length may be more effective in handling their tasks.
5   Another key theme is to make agencies focus upon results, for instance, through the use of so-called executive agencies.
6   The logic of agencies is the quid pro quo equation: do agencies produce more value than their costs?

Suggested readings

Flinders, M.V. and M.J. Smith (eds) (1998) *Quangos, Accountability and Reform: The Politics of Quasi-Government*. Basingstoke: Palgrave Macmillan.

Gains, F. (2003) "Executive Agencies in Government: The Impact of Bureaucratic Networks on Policy Outcomes", *Journal of Public Policy*, Vol. 23, No. 1: 55–79.

Greve, C., M. Flinders, S. Van Thiel (1999) "Quangos – What's in a Name? Defining Quangos from a Comparative Perspective", *Governance*, Vol. 12, No. 2: 129–146.

Hedberg, B.L.T., P.C. Nystrom and W.H. Starbuck (1976) "Camping on Seesaws: Prescriptions for a Self-Designing Organization", *Administrative Science Quarterly*, Vol. 21: 41–65.

Hogwood, B.W. (1995) "The 'Growth' of Quangos: Evidence and Explanations", *Parliamentary Affairs*, Vol. 48: 207–225.

Hogwood, B.W. (1995) "Whitehall Families: Core Departments and Agency Forms", *International Review of Administrative Sciences*, Vol. 61: 511–530.

Hood, C., O. James, B.G. Peters and C. Scott (eds) (2005) *Controlling Modern Government: Variety, Commonality and Change*. Cheltenham: Edward Elgar.

James, O. (2004) *The Executive Agency Revolution in Whitehall: Public Interest Versus Bureau-Shaping Perspectives*. Basingstoke: Palgrave Macmillan.

Kaufman, H. (1991) *Time, Chance and Organizations: Natural Selection in a Perilous Environment*. Chatham, NJ: Chatham House.

Pollitt, C., J. Caulfield, A. Smullen and C. Talbot (2004) *Agencies: How Governments Do Things Through Semi-autonomous Organizations*. Basingstoke: Palgrave Macmillan.

Talbot, C. (2004) "Executive Agencies: Have They Improved Management in Government?", *Public Money and Management*, Vol. 24, No. 2: 104–112.

Thynne, I. (2003) "Making Sense of Organizations in Public Management: A Back-to Basics Approach", *Public Organization Review*, Vol. 3, No. 3: 317–332.

Wettenhall, R. (2005) "Agencies and Non-Departmental Public Bodies: The Hard and Soft Lenses of Agencification Theory", *Public Management Review*, Vol. 7, No. 4: 615–635.

Web resources

http://www.nuffield.ox.ac.uk/Politics/Whitehall/Machinery.html (last accessed on 13/11/2008).

http://en.wikipedia.org/wiki/QUANGO (last accessed on 13/11/2008).

6 Policy network models

The virtues and vices of public–private partnerships

Introduction

State management is not confined to bureaucrats or public agencies, as it touches upon the interests of private actors and third sector people. If they are concerned with public policies and how policies are implemented, then why not include them somehow in public management? This idea, which flows in a natural way from broadening the perspective of public management from formal organisation or bureaucracy to informal patterns of behaviour, was developed into a major framework of public management after the implementation gap had been discovered and recognised. Policy networks would comprise several public organisations having a stake in some programmes, but also private actors or third sector organisations.

Public management as networks of people or as public–private partnerships became a major approach in the 1990s. It had roots in the literature on interest intermediation as well as in Dutch innovations in service delivery. Thus, one finds the theory about the importance of broad society participation in policy-making and implementation in notions of co-governance. But it was developed into a coherent framework for public management especially by Dutch scholars, linking the delivery of public services with the emergence of a strong civil society in advanced democratic countries.

Different modes of public and private cooperation

When public management is to be based upon a partnership between the public and private sectors, then one distinguishes between three forms of cooperation: co-governance, co-management and co-production (Public Management Review, 2006).

Corporatism: the social economy

Public administration reaching out to set up structures of collaboration with the private sector has had a long standing in countries where corporatism is well entrenched and accepted. Thus, one finds in the Scandinavian countries such as Finland, and also in Austria, formal mechanisms for the participation of organised interests in policy-making and implementation. Corporatist interest intermediation includes a number of devices: representation in public boards, responsibility for enforcing rules, co-determination and consultation schemes, public hearing activities and tax relief for membership dues (Crouch and Streeck, 2006).

Corporatist structures may occur at various levels of government, both at the top and at the bottom. Famous corporatist schemes include the administration of unemployment compensation in Sweden, the management of fishing quotas in Norway, and industrial policy-making in Austria besides the often-occurring co-determination institutions in the bigger private firms.

Corporatism animated a hot debate about the central issue, namely, whether private interests can be given a quasi-formal role in the administration of public affairs. The adherents argued that corporatist networks enhanced political stability and social trust, while the detractors maintained that they lacked public legitimacy and could be employed for rent-seeking purposes. How, then, are general networks like any public–private partnership to be evaluated?

British network governance research

British network scholars have argued with considerable effort, albeit not always in a coherent manner, that public–private partnership is the way of the future (Rhodes, 2007). On the one hand, it is argued – critically – that the network model results in the hollowing out of the state. But on the other hand, it is suggested – positively – that network governance presents a flexible and efficient work unit that may compensate for the cut-back of bureaucratic size.

The vast reforms of the British state cannot be reduced to network governance. They included other types of reform measures such agencification, NPM, incorporation and privatisation. Yet, networks for the delivery of public services were introduced, especially outside of Whitehall (Goss, 2001). In British research, network governance could refer to either collaboration between governments at various levels or the formation of implementation groups including private people or non-governmental organisations. It seems to me that the proper definition of network governance is the public–private partnership, which tends to be mostly horizontal in nature. Vertical forms of interaction are better subsumed under the theory of multi-level governance.

Dutch network theory: public–private partnerships

The theory that policy networks are the best forms of public management and not merely one alternative mechanism for public service delivery was launched by a number of Dutch scholars. It built, no doubt, upon a country-specific legacy of pooling resources, public and private, when attacking a problem like, for instance, the management of water. But the Dutch scholars insisted that the policy networks would result in effective public management everywhere (Kooiman, 2003; Kickert, 1997; Rhodes, 1997). The policy network idea would not have had such success in public management had it not been the case that it was well in tune with other popular ideas such as social capital and trust.

Public management as a network of people collaborating in the delivery of services takes into account the role of informal organisation as well as the importance of street-level bureaucrats. The quality of public management being a function of information and reward of incentives, the policy network approach offers a decentralised framework for meeting the knowledge requirements. People really interested in the service in question come together to share their different experiences. Since each participant in a network is driven by a strong personal ambition to perform well, new knowledge will automatically be searched for. The network breaks down hierarchy and compartmentalisation, allowing people with different professional experiences to share in a common effort. The network framework accords well with the general movement towards a flatter hierarchy and the empowerment of lower level employees. It can also draw heavily upon the information revolution in the form of the internet society.

A policy network may consist of any people who have an interest in the public service in question, whatever their job situation may be. Thus, policy networks score high on organisational flexibility. They may bring in people from civil society where so many NGOs harbour highly motivated persons with lots of relevant knowledge. They may also contract with persons having special expertise, offering assistance for a limited period of time.

The Dutch preference for network governance originated in the historical success of Dutch water management policies (Kickert *et al.*, 1997). The relevance of the network approach can be generalised to any policy area where information would be forthcoming in a decentralised manner and where individual incentives to make a contribution to the whole play a major role (Koppenjan and Klijn, 2004). Thus, networks would be successful, comparatively speaking, when technology is ill-defined and there is strong interdependency among the actors at the same time.

Networks in governance: pros and cons

The popularity of the network model derives from several sources. First, it fits well with a bottom-up approach to policy implementation. Second, it is in tune with the internet revolution or the use of new information and communication technologies that favour horizontal interaction. Third, it renders a place for civil society in policy implementation and public sector activities. Finally, it acknowledges that successful policy-making depends upon policy awareness or learning in evolving policy environments where peoples' motivation plays a major role, not only that of bureaucrats or professionals but also that of the stakeholders. It seems to me that the network model when interpreted in public–private partnerships could be useful for policy implementation in certain contexts, but it is not a panacea removing the implementation gap.

What is not clear in the theory of policy networks is the role of incentives. Thus, one may ask how these networks reward incentives as well as who decides the main goals of the group. Network theory tends to leave these crucial questions for public management aside, assuming somehow that highly motivated people will automatically do their best and that the main objectives of such groups are somehow given.

The creation of quangos in the UK and the use of policy networks in the Netherlands led many countries to experiment with this model of public management, although on a smaller scale. The debate on the advantages and disadvantages of public management as quangos or policy networks focusses almost exclusively upon the incentives in such groups. While acknowledging that they may score high on the access to and employment of relevant information, the framework is criticised for murky goals. How can government be sure that the networks really implement government policy?

The Achilles heel of the policy network approach is that questions of accountability and responsibility are difficult to address. These networks may become so independent that they are impossible to control or govern. And how is the question of proper remuneration to be solved, when these groups exercise considerable discretion and autonomy?

Networks do not, in general, replace agencies, but they may operate extremely well with the delivery of certain kinds of public services, namely, social care such as old age care, for instance. When there is a strong private or third sector interest in having certain services delivered, then networks offer suitable institutional arrangements. For instance, water level management and fresh water regulation is not only a vital concern for the various governments at different levels but also for farmers and community groups. Another example is the interest in charitable organisations in helping to provide social care.

Networks may also be the best institutional arrangement when technology is uncertain and spread out on many hands. Thus, networks in preventive social care as well as in complicated infrastructure projects make sense. But networks cannot replace the bureaucratic organisation of ministries, departments, universities or local governments.

The key question: policy networks and incentives

Public management as networks fits well with the recent emphasis upon social capital and the role of civil society. Why could not government use third sector organisations in the delivery of many public services? Since networks are malleable and fungible, they enhance flexibility and adaptation in government. It is stated that trust is the cement that holds the policy network together (Bryce, 2005). Several so-called factors of confidence may be identified behind public management as networks:

1   In a non-profit, trust is derived from the convergence of interests in serving a clientele;
2   A non-profit will respect its legal mission;
3   A non-profit can attract donations;
4   A non-profit generates goodwill, adding to social capital.

Yet, people who work in networks are not saints. They will lobby for their personal interests in good working conditions and a stable pattern of organisational dominance. Networks may simply serve to generate income for third sector organisations while at the same time not being strictly accountable to anyone.

Setting up and running a network for the delivery of public services poses a set of elementary questions concerning any team that is supposed to deliver these services. These problems cannot be avoided by assuming that a network resolves them simply by being called "network". In reality, these questions involve the economic and political fundamentals of these teams, such as:

1   *Remuneration*: people in networks must be paid, which raises the questions of the quid pro quo between effort, results and salary.
2   *Results*: networks are only worthwhile if they deliver outputs as well as outcomes, meaning that they have to be evaluated with the possibility of termination.
3   *Responsibility*: in a team of people there has to be coordination. As it is not likely to be forthcoming in a spontaneous manner, some form of structure must be imposed upon the network.

4 *Accountability*: While it is true that power may be dispersed in a network of people, the network itself must answer to outsiders (government, the press) about its achievements.
5 *Complaint*: As long as the network delivers a *public* service, there must be a possibility for a client to express a complaint about its operations.

These aspects of networks must be considered important ones, as they refer to their daily conduct of activities. Sooner or later networks in a constitutional democracy will be called upon to answer questions relating to them. Yet, in the English and Dutch literature on networks these aspects are not given the importance that their relevance calls for.

Conclusion

As soon as one abandons the idea that public management must be the sole preoccupation of bureaux or agencies under the direct control of a government (central, regional, local), then one may, by and by, arrive at the other extreme, namely, that public management is basically people in interaction. Once the planning framework is also given up, one would be inclined to find adequate information about the technology of delivering public services in a decentralised approach. Public management as policy networks combines therein two seminal developments away from bureaucracy and centralisation. If the quality of policy implementation really depends upon the lower levels in the hierarchy, then why not empower people producing the public services to participate in *ad hoc* groups with stakeholders from the private sector and society? Surely, information will increase, but what about goals and incentives?

The negative side of policy networks is often stated with the economist's terms: "capture", "collusion", "rent-seeking" and "special interests". The basic idea is that groups may start with an orientation towards public interest but develop more and more towards the protection of narrow interests, their own or those of major private stakeholders such as organised interests. Klijn and Koppenjan, writing several articles claiming that networks are the best institutional structure for delivering public services in the post-modern society, do not really solve the crucial problem of quid pro quo in public–private partnerships: is cost always proportionate to delivery? If not, how is that corrected?

There is more to public management than merely setting up a policy network. Starting from the questions about how these units operate, and how they are to be held accountable, one would like to know how the internal governance is handled in such groups as well as how they respond to the call for transparency and efficiency from their principal, e.g. the national government.

Thus, a policy network could not possibly be self-sufficient, as there would have to be public monitoring of performance as well as regulation in order to offer citizens the avenue of redress. Looking at agents in terms of networks comprising public and private employees as well as stakeholders only makes the application of the principal–agent framework more complex, but not redundant.

Essential summary

1   The notion of networks is a popular response to increasing complexity in state management and growing dependency upon civil society.
2   A network could be a horizontal team of people working for the implementation of a set of objectives, related to policy.
3   Networks typically involve public–private partnerships, constituting flexible teams with considerable knowledge about local conditions for implementation.
4   The incentive problem in state management is more easily solvable in a network, as private individuals may draw upon their willingness to contribute and interest in effective implementation.
5   The steering problem is more difficult to handle in a public–private partnership, as private individuals may not accept the requirements of coordination easily. It may be difficult to identify the border of a policy network.
6   The non-profit organisation is a new partner in networks, which may contribute both motivation and information to the process of policy implementation.

Suggested readings

Berman, E.M. (2006) *Performance and Productivity in Public and Nonprofit Organizations*. Armonk, NY: M.E. Sharpe.

Bryce, H.J. (2005) *Players in the Public Policy Process: Nonprofits as Social Capital and Agents*. Basingstoke: Palgrave Macmillan.

Crouch, C. and W. Streeck (eds) (2006) *The Diversity of Democracy: Corporatism, Social Order and Political Conflict*. Cheltenham: Edward Elgar.

Goss, S. (2001) *Making Local Governance Work: Networks, Relationships and the Management of Change*. Basingstoke: Palgrave Macmillan.

Gunn, C. (2004) *Third-Sector Development: Making Up for the Market*. Ithaca, NY: Cornell University Press.

Kickert, W.J.M (1997) "Public Governance in the Netherlands: An Alternative to Anglo-American 'Managerialism'", *Public Administration*, Vol. 75, No. 4: 731–752.

Kickert, W.J.M., E.-H. Klijn and J.F.M. Koppenjan (1997) *Managing Complex Networks: Strategies for the Public Sector*. London: SAGE Publications.

Knoke, D., F.U. Pappi, J. Broadbent, Y. Tsujinaka (1996) *Comparing Policy Networks: Labor Politics in the U.S., Germany, and Japan* (Cambridge Studies in Comparative Politics), Cambridge: Cambridge University Press.

Kooiman, J. (2003) *Governing as Governance*. London: SAGE Publications.

Koppenjan, J. and E.-H. Klijn (2004) *Managing Uncertainties in Networks: Public–Private Controversies*. London: Routledge.

Marcussen, M. and J. Torfing (eds) (2006) *Democratic Network Governance in Europe*. Basingstoke: Palgrave Macmillan.

Public Management Review (2006) *Special Issue: Co-production: The Third Sector and the Delivery of Public Services*, Vol. 8, No. 4.

Rhodes, R.A.W. (1997) *Understanding Governance: Policy Networks, Governance, Reflexivity and Accountability*. Milton Keynes: Open University Press.

7 Marketisation models
How much should government use internal markets and public procurement?

Introduction

Public management and government are often considered as different faces of the same thing, namely, authority. Government enacts decisions, laws and budgets, and it employs agencies to put them into practice, whether it is called "execution" or "implementation". Modern government relies upon legal-rational authority, stated Weber. And as long as public management was approached in terms of formal organisation and planning, it was basically true that it was, in essence, the exercise of authority.

Yet, with new approaches to public management this equation of public management = authority is no longer helpful. When public management is handled through decentralised or deconcentrated government, or entrusted to quangos and policy networks, then public management is *not*, first and foremost, the exercise of authority. Public management is the governance of teams that deliver services. And this governance may employ alternative methods of coordination: authority, market and trust.

The idea that government could get the job done through buying and selling entailed a revolution in the thinking about public management. Public management as so-called internal markets added to the tools of government (Hood and Margetts, 2007), whether it took the extreme form of compulsive competitive tendering under Thatcher or merely constituted a convenient way to reduce costs in public service delivery.

Tendering/bidding

Government always has to pick up the costs for running agencies that deliver public services. Costs can easily be quantified and never be avoided. What is enigmatic in public management is the value of the services delivered, since they are not sold and bought in a market. Yet, government would always wish to pay less, all other things being equal. Thus, if the same services could be delivered at a lower cost, then government could save money or spend it elsewhere.

Cost explosions for public services have occurred now and then in many countries. Most of the costs are salaries, or roughly 70 per cent in an average program, and they tend almost always to move upwards with inflation and trade union power. Traditional public administration developed a number of strategies to contain costs within the framework of budget allocation from a Ministry of Finance, such as:

1   systematic cost comparisons between agencies;
2   general cost reductions over all programmes;
3   amalgamations of agencies in order to find synergies.

Generally speaking, traditional public administration was not very successful in containing costs. Instead, the constant expansion of the public sector since the end of the Second World War stimulated a debate about the impossibility of containing costs in public administration. The Ministry of Finance did send out its spies by means of an Audit Bureau, but public sector growth seemed unstoppable. Very controversial models like the Parkinson bureau growth model or the Niskanen bureau maximising model entailed that the public agency faced a principled problem with costs, as it could not put the brakes upon their growth.

The traditional bureau as framed in administrative law according to the Weberian approach to bureaucracy concealed that the delivery of public services always has two sides: demand for the service and the supply of the same service. The public bureau used to be run by a political board that somehow both ordered and provided the services in question. Thus, a public university would not merely offer a package of services to the Ministry of Finance, but it would also try to make sure that the money-allocating authority demanded the best mix of university programmes.

The same mix of demand and supply occurred in the government itself. On the one hand, the various ministries and the agencies under their authority supplied lots of services or programmes. But at the same time, the ministries were to be judges of which services and programmes were to be given priority. How can there be cost efficiency when the demanding agent is more or less also the supplying agent? Under the classical bureau model, government as demand preferences would always be entangled into the interests of government as supply.

Public management as tendering/bidding was launched as a method to break this conflation of demand and supply in the public sector. It was systematically developed in the so-called New Zealand model and adopted with great consequences in both Australia and the UK. The idea was to insert a market-like competitive mechanism into the public sector. Government would tender what services it wished to provide and then proceed to choose among alternative service providers, bidding for the contract. Now, government had always been conducting such tendering/bidding procedures for a limited number of projects, such as infrastructure and renovation of buildings. What was new in the New Zealand model and with Thatcherism was the scale to which tendering/bidding was to be put into effect.

The crux of the matter is that when tendering/bidding is launched on such a grand scale as in the public sector reforms in the 1980s, then it has massive organisational consequences. The structure of classical bureaux cannot be upheld. As the new philosophy of tendering/bidding gained momentum in public management, bureaucracy came under increasing pressure. In some countries, the bureaucracy at the central level of government was reformed drastically.

Tendering/bidding and cost efficiency are linked to each other through powerful theorems in economics, such as Walras' competitive equilibrium. The move to underline tendering/bidding was, in fact, part of a general political ideology that wanted to halt public sector growth and if possible reduce public expenditures with the exception of military outlays – the neo-conservative wave. However, the tendering/bidding strategy for public management was also adopted by governments with a social democratic leaning. It was seen as a tool for really coming to grips with strong internal forces that pushed costs up year in and year out. And it could prove very effective against strong trade unions, demanding high wage increases all the time.

Public management as tendering/bidding puts the emphasis not upon hierarchy in formal organisation but upon contract. Contract making can deliver efficient solutions under certain conditions, outlined in standard courses in microeconomics. The key thing is to mimic these in public management. If that could be done, then allocative efficiency would result automatically from contracting, reducing unit costs and closing down inefficient units. The standard model of contracting is the so-called Edgeworth box, demonstrating how fully informed actors reach a set of Pareto-optimal contracts. Unique solutions to bargaining were handed down in the Rubinstein model of negotiation.

Tendering/bidding when introduced on a major scale implies both wide-ranging organisational changes and the introduction of a new technique of governance, namely, contracting out and contracting in. The requirement of transparency in government called for proper procedures of tendering and bidding, especially if the country in question was a member of the EU or the WTO. The general model for comprehensive tendering/bidding that emerged from Compulsive Competitive Tendering in the UK and local government restructuring in Scandinavia is referred to as "internal markets", a phrase which signifies a lot about the effort to replace bureaucracy.

Internal markets: buyers and sellers

There are, in principle, only two ways to create market allocation for so-called public services. One either privatises the service entirely or one sets up a market-like mechanism in the public sector. It is the latter strategy that is pursued when agencies are replaced by internal markets.

The general model of public management as internal market splits the agency into one board tendering and buying, as well as a set of providers, bidding and receiving contracts. The model is also called the "purchaser–provider" split. Between these two – buyers and sellers – there is the process of tendering, bidding, screening and, finally, selection of the winners of contract. In principle, there is no limit upon the entry of various bidders, as they can be public agencies, private firms, third sector organisations or merely private individuals. The key point is, of course, that the bureau loses its classical position, meaning monopoly, tenure and expertise. It can tender for contracts but it is not given any special consideration when contracts are awarded.

Internal markets are clearly feasible. Government has enough money to instruct a purchasing board of managers to tender for the delivery of public services. This tendering process can be made regional, as with the EU, or international, as with the WTO. Bidders will be forthcoming under normal circumstances, at least with bids from the public agencies that lost their monopoly. Contracts will be awarded for a shorter period of say 2–4 years, after which the tendering/bidding process will be renewed. Such procedures are well known in the theory of public procurement and in the theory of auctions. The problem with the internal market model is the scope of its application. When done in an encompassing fashion, it will give rise to certain costs, called "transaction costs".

Advantages and disadvantages of internal markets

The introduction of internal markets on a grand scale could only be done as part of a political revolution – the neo-conservative or neo-liberal wave of the 1980s. It uproots bureaucracy and challenges the trade unions. Thus, it requires a strong political mandate and firm political determination to see through reforms that change employment massively.

The internal market philosophy was resented by those who stood to lose: bureaucrats, professionals and public employees with some sort of tenure. It was opposed by trade unions, fearing job losses among their members. Yet, the critical question is: can tendering/bidding be made to work for all kinds of public services? If so, then what are the gains from introducing such schemes of public management?

First, the generalisability of the internal market is questionable. This model of public management seems to fit certain services but not others. The crux of the matter is the extent to which a service can be fully contracted in all its aspects. The more standardised and quantitative the service is, the more suitable it is for the internal market. And the opposite also holds true: the more qualitative the service and the less it can be specified in a contract, the more unsuitable it is for the internal market. Several services in the core public sector are truly soft, and their delivery involves strong personal commitment. How can they be allocated efficiently in a tendering/bidding process?

The internal market scheme was to be used on all kinds of services at all levels of government, including the public enterprises. Setting up a regime of tendering/bidding for the traditional public enterprises included several major reforms of them and their regulation, to be examined in the next chapter. It was feasible to arrive at a liberalised market for products like electricity, natural gas and waste disposal, sometimes in terms of a regional regulatory regime. However, services like child care, disability assistance, old age care and mental counselling do not really fit the internal market model. There are a couple of restrictions upon its use, including the following:

(1) *Asset-specific knowledge*: Asset specificity is usually defined as the extent to which the investments made to support a particular transaction have a higher value to that transaction than they would have if they were redeployed for any other purpose. When there are asset-specific competences in the provision of public services, then marketisation may fail and internal organisation is to be preferred. The production of a certain component may require investment in specialised equipment, the distribution of a certain product may necessitate unique physical facilities, or the delivery of a certain service may be predicated on the existence of an uncommon set of professional know-how and skills.

Asset specificity occurs in a typical buyer–seller situation, where the buyer is the party that does not hold the specific assets and the seller is the party that holds the specific assets. At first, the hold-up was modelled as unilateral: the buyer holds up the seller. However, later researchers have realised that asset specificity could be bilateral, or even multi-lateral. In a traditional buyer–seller situation, the hold-up could be bilateral, because the buyer (the party that does not hold the specific assets) has exit cost associated with time and searching for investment if he decides to switch party.

(2) *Transaction costs*: These costs are incurred in any trading of goods or services. A mutually beneficial trade requires one to find out that there may be someone with whom such a trade is feasible, as well as searching out possible trade partners, informing him/them of the opportunity, and negotiating the

terms of the exchange - activities having opportunity costs in terms of time, energy and money. In public provision, one should not make the simplifying assumption that transaction costs are zero. In marketisation, the benefits to the participants in an exchange have to be high enough to cover their transaction costs. Several mutually advantageous trades may not take place due to considerable transaction costs that would be involved. Internal organisation may be preferable. In transaction cost economics, one takes into account not only the opportunity costs *ex ante* a deal or a contract but also the opportunity costs that may have to be incurred *ex post* in order to validate and enforce the contract (http://en.wikipedia.org/wiki/Transaction_cost). It is actually difficult to tell exactly which costs are to be counted as transaction costs. One finds both narrow and wide definitions in the literature (Furubotn and Richter, 2005), but the following costs are typically included: search and information costs incurred in determining whether the good or service is available on the market, which has the lowest price, etc; bargaining costs incurred to come to an acceptable agreement with the other party to the transaction, outlining an appropriate contract and so on. In game theory this is analysed, for example, in the game of battle of the sexes. Enforcement costs of making sure the other party sticks to the terms of the contract, perhaps of taking appropriate legal action, are also included. Transaction costs can be widened to also cover institutional costs, but then the concept becomes vague. In reality, transaction costs are related to fungibility, i.e. the property of units of economic exchange to be easily exchangeable. Its individual units are capable of mutual substitution: different instances/units of the same type of unit make no difference.

Public procurement

Little theorised, public procurement has always been one of the tools of government. Several countries used to have a central agency that was responsible for the buying of equipment to bureaux. It had detailed instructions from governments how to go about buying things at home or abroad. In public procurement it is market skills that count.

Recently, public procurement has received more attention, especially when a regional body like the European Union has created a regional market for government purchases. Many departments and bureaux now have their own procurement procedures, although government often wishes to instruct them to pay as low as possible meaning that they should search for competitive supplies. In the United States, outhouse production was always larger than in Europe, meaning that public procurement was a standard feature of government. As in-house production has been reduced in Europe, more attention has been paid to the problematic of public procurement.

Public procurement has two sides. First, there is the question of institutions or rules to be followed. In the context of the European Union, there is one set of rules for all public procurement whether by central, regional or local governments, handled by Brussels through one central tendering/bidding system. Thus, over a certain level of purchase, governments must tender the contracts to be allocated on the European Union website. Second, there is the problem of maximising the gains in procurement, taking into account all the costs – production costs and transaction costs (Laffont and Tirole, 1993).

The relevance of understanding public procurement has increased for several reasons. Let me mention a few:

1   increasing scale of public capital projects;
2   growing international competition for public contract;
3   harmonisation of the rules for tendering and bidding for public capital projects;
4   the transformation from in-house production to outhouse provision.

Public procurement ranges from giant projects like airport constructions to mini projects such as buying of computers. There is lots of money to be gained from opening up national public procurement to regional or international competition. Often, a country does not possess the competence necessary for big infrastructure projects, which must be tendered regionally or internationally. Public procurement invites opportunistic behaviour, which can only be countered by means of the enforcement of clear rules in a transparent manner. Finally, public procurement is close to the philosophy of the internal market with NPM, although in principle, public procurement deals with huge investment projects.

The central problem: production costs against transaction costs

Public management as internal markets, or the design of processes of tendering and bidding, has to solve the thorny question of balancing the advantages and disadvantages of this form of service delivery against other forms. It is a matter for relative institutional evaluation, attempting to find the cut-off point where internal markets become a drag on government. The general solution to this question has been suggested by Oliver Williamson and the so-called economic theory of organisation, first outlined by Coase.

Government would be well advised to engage in tendering and bidding as the mechanism for public service delivery, when:

1   transaction costs are low;
2   there is competition in supply forthcoming;

3   no asset-specific knowledge is made public;
4   opportunism can be handled.

Williamson posited a general distinction between so-called hierarchies, i.e. organisation with internal production, and markets, i.e. buying and selling in a competitive environment. Assuming a general drive towards reducing costs, private companies mix hierarchy and markets on the basis of relative cost comparisons between in-house production (low transaction costs) and outhouse production (high transaction costs). Competition in supply would reduce production costs, but the costs of negotiating outhouse production as well as monitoring the respect for contracts must be added to the equation. The same logic applies to government when it makes a choice between traditional bureau supply on the one hand and a tendering/ bidding process on the other hand.

Besides the minimisation of overall costs (production costs and transaction costs), Williamson suggests that incentives to the players affect the choice of organisational form or institutional design. Thus, opportunism on the part of the supplier is a negative for external organisation, whereas the possession of asset-specific knowledge with the supplier is a positive for internal organisation (Williamson and Masten, 1999).

Conclusion

Public management as buying and selling had been a small concern of government within its procurement activities. When engaged in on a major scale, it required far-reaching organisational changes, labelled the "internal market". Whereas public procurement has been an ongoing activity within government, requiring regional and international regulation when the size of the contracts becomes truly large, the internal market strategy was revolutionary. It definitely broke the spell of bureaucracy over public organisation.

Instead of the issuing of commands, public management becomes the handling of contracts: tendering, screening, selection and monitoring of contract proposals. Whether government is contracting *in* or contracting *out*, it has a high chance of making efficient deals, especially if there are many potential service providers, or bidders for contracts. It is choice and competition replacing authority and monopoly.

Yet, when it is argued that government can employ buying and selling almost universally (Osborne and Plastrik, 1998), then we have an exaggeration that is dangerous for government. Contracting out is not a panacea against all budgetary crises, fiscal deficits and bureaucratic inefficiencies. Government will still want to use its public law arm, since it gives it the power to command. In reality, tendering/bidding and contracting out is an option for government that it may consider using in combination with its power as a public authority.

Essential summary

1   A major reform in state management, stimulated by the emergence of New Public Management, is the introduction of market-like mechanisms in the allocation of goods and services.
2   Under the label of "internal markets", public sector reform outlined how government may employ the mechanisms of tendering and bidding to effect policy implementation.
3   "Marketisation" would include both privatisation, contracting out and contracting in.
4   Governments have always used procurement techniques. What NPM suggested was to use them on a grand scale, possibly for all services: market-testing devices.
5   A theory of transaction costs may help our understanding of the limits of marketisation strategies.

Suggested readings

Boston, J. (2000) "Organizing for Service Delivery: Criteria and Opportunities", in B.G. Peters and D. Savoie (eds) *Governance in the Twenty-first Century: Revitalizing Public Services*. Montreal: McGill-Queen's University Press, 281–331.

Boston, J., P. Dalziel and S. St. John (eds) (1999) *Redesigning the Welfare State in New Zealand*. Auckland: Oxford University Press.

Brown, K. and S.P. Osborne (2005) *Managing Change and Innovation in Public Service Organizations*. London: Routledge.

Ferlie, E., L.E. Lynn and C. Pollit (eds) (2007) *The Oxford Handbook of Public Management*. Oxford: Oxford University Press.

Furubotn, E.G. and R. Richter (2005) *Institutions and Economic Theory*. Ann Arbor: University of Michigan Press.

Hood, C. and H. Margetts (2007) *The Tools of Government in the Digital Age*. London: Palgrave Macmillan.

Laffont, J.-J. and J. Tirole (1993) *A Theory of Incentives in Procurement and Regulation*. Cambridge, MA: The MIT Press.

McLaughlin, K., S.P. Osborne and E. Ferlie (eds) (2001) *The New Public Management: Current Trends and Future Prospects*. London: Routledge.

Osborne, D. and P. Plastrik (1998) *Banishing Bureaucracy: The Five Strategies for Reinventing Government*. New York: Plume Books.

Pyper, R. and A. Massey (2005) *Public Management and Modernisation in Britain*. Basingstoke: Palgrave Macmillan.

Williamson, O.E. and S.E. Masten (eds) (1999) *The Economics of Transaction Costs*. Cheltenham: Edward Elgar.

8 Incorporation as a strategy
Transforming the public enterprises

Introduction

Nowhere has the change in public management been more far-reaching, comprehensive and coherent than in the part of the public sector made up of so-called trading departments (Thynne, 1994). Public enterprises have all been transformed, both internally in their organisation structure, and externally, i.e. in the market setting that they are placed in. The traditional public enterprise is no longer in existence. It has been transformed into a public joint-stock company, which constitutes an organisational form that may also be used outside of the so-called business sector.

The business sector harbouring the public firms that sell their goods to the public with charges or user fees is large, in whatever manner it is organised. It comprises huge enterprises with infrastructure having massive capital expenditures and investments. Some of them are also very big employers. Thus, the economic impact of public enterprises is quite substantial. The neo-liberal wave had drastic implications for the traditional public enterprise as a result of deregulation and incorporation. As the entire field of infrastructure was reformed as a result of liberalisation, the trading department had to be transformed into a joint-stock company in order to be able to act in a competitive market nationally, regionally and internationally.

The classical European and American models

The goods and services in infrastructure may be provided by either public firms, as in Europe, or by public utilities, as in the United States. Public utilities are privately owned firms that operate within a regulatory frame, decided by state or local governments. The European public enterprise was a bureaucracy with the rights to do business within a narrow framework, controlled by the Ministry of Finance. Its official purpose was to provide cheap goods and services, even if it was loss-making. But its unofficial goal was often to provide employment, thus reducing unemployment.

Both the European public enterprise and the American public utility operated under a regulatory regime that restricted entry while negotiating the price of the goods and services. Thus, these firms were basically monopolies but had their charges or rates set by government, or a regulatory agency. Also, the European public enterprise had to have government approval for raising its rates, but they were in any case run more or less from the Ministry of Finance. The European public enterprise especially had huge numbers of employees, which sometimes led to an accusation of inefficiency.

Traditional public regulation was often motivated by reference to so-called sunk costs, i.e. costs that have already been incurred and which cannot be recovered to any significant degree. Sunk costs are sometimes contrasted with variable costs, which are the costs that will change due to the proposed course of action. Investments in infrastructure tend to be huge, and thus they can only be recovered over a long period of time when the producer may need supranatural profits in order to write off huge capital investments. Thus, competition should be limited by means of licences. Yet, in microeconomic theory, only variable costs are relevant to a decision. Rational actors do not let sunk costs influence decisions, because doing so would not be assessing a decision exclusively on its own merits.

The liberalisation wave changed all of this, as infrastructure was opened up with free entry in principle. The regulatory regime was changed or abolished. The change of the setting was based upon a new theory of regulation – capture theory, which argued that efficiency will only be forthcoming if there is deregulation. Public management for public enterprises must target the key parameters in bringing about a deregulated market where free entry would lead to low prices and large quantities of goods and services. In a deregulated market, the public enterprise would face intruders, public or private. There would be competition in regional markets or on the international scene. Thus, deregulation induced changes in the organisation of the public firm. It could no longer be a trading department as a bureau within the Ministry of Finance. As it had to face competitors, it needed a governance structure that facilitated quick decisions and company profitability, i.e. incorporation as a strategy was born.

As a result of deregulation and privatisation, one may say that Europe has also adopted the public utilities model. The only difference is that in Europe the state remains a major owner of equity in these joint-stock companies whereas this is not the case with American public utilities. Basically, there are no traditional trading departments or public enterprises left in Europe. Yet, many big infrastructure firms remain in state hands, although they are incorporated and run like any joint-stock company.

Use of private law in public management

The transformation of the public enterprises in the wake of the deregulation wave was called "incorporation" by Ian Thynne. It is a most adequate term for vast changes in organisation and strategy. Although government had earlier owned stock in various private companies, either for industrial policy reasons or merely because the company in question went bankrupt, it was the scale of the incorporation drive that was stunning. All kinds of public enterprises have been incorporated: railways, postal services, water and sewage, electricity and gas, as well as telecommunications. And in some cases, there was sometimes, in addition, partial or total privatisation.

The joint-stock company falls under private law, whereas the traditional public enterprise as a bureau used to be run according to public law. The almost complete endorsement of the joint-stock company as the organisational frame for running a public firm has contributed most significantly to the diversification of public management. Accepting the joint-stock company format implies a restriction of the scope of politics and an increase in the range of business as usual. The pace of transformation was very quick, sometimes leading to the full-scale privatisation of huge enterprises. Complete privatisation involved, of course, a considerable shrinking of the public sector, but mere incorporation changed the entire way in which the public enterprises were managed.

The status of employees was altered when private law replaced public law. The public enterprises sought to increase their efficiency in a deregulated market by shedding labour, a strategy which has made it easier to engage with the joint-stock company. Joint-stock companies must maintain their equity and cannot show negative results year in and year out. As a shareholder, it is easier to deny new capital and demand cost savings than when the firm is a bureau under administrative law. Public management as incorporation was used as a global strategy in order to create competition in infrastructure and make public firms more profitable and less loss-making.

Public management and corporate governance

The application of the joint-stock firm as a framework for an organisation is not confined to the proper business sector. It can also be extended to comprise teams of people working in the soft sector. Thus, incorporation may be used in the health care sector when it is subjected to the internal market regime. Although local governments and universities are sometimes called "corporations", state management as incorporation entails the use of the special economic corporation that private law singles out as the joint-stock company.

Advantages

The chief advantage of the incorporated organisation is flexibility and a clear focus upon business. As an incorporated economic unity, it has to maintain its capital. Thus, losses every year will eventually lead to the elimination of the company, or bankruptcy. The owners of the company do not assume more risk than the capital they have put up – i.e. they have limited liability. Moreover, the corporation, having the status of a legal person, can decide for itself what to do in a rapidly changing environment.

A corporation requires a special legal framework and body of law that specifically grants the corporation legal personality, and typically views a corporation as a *fictional person* or a *legal person*. Corporate statutes provide corporations with the ability to own property, sign binding contracts and pay taxes, having a capacity to take decisions that is separate from its shareholders.

For instance, a corporation grants creditors priority over the corporate assets upon liquidation, but corporate assets cannot be withdrawn by its shareholders. The assets of the firm can normally not be taken by personal creditors of its shareholders. The institutions most favourable to incorporation include the following (http://en.wikipedia.org/wiki/Corporation; http://en.wikipedia.org/wiki/Limited_liability; http://en.wikipedia.org/wiki/Venture_Capital):

Limited liability   Unlike in a partnership or sole proprietorship, shareholders of a modern business corporation have "limited" liability for the corporation's debts and obligations. As a result, their potential losses cannot exceed the amount which they contributed to the corporation as dues or paid for shares. Limited liability allows anonymous trading in the shares of the corporation by virtue of eliminating the corporation's creditors as a stakeholder in such a transaction. Limited liability further allows corporations to raise funds for enterprises by combining funds from the owners of stock. Since limited liability reduces the amount that a shareholder can lose in a company, the risk for potential shareholders is reduced, which increases both the number of willing shareholders and the amount they are likely to invest.

Perpetual lifetime   The assets and structure of the corporation exist beyond the lifetime of any of its shareholders, bondholders, or employees. This allows for accumulation of capital, which thus becomes available for investment in projects of a larger size and over a longer term than if the corporate assets remained subject to dissolution and distribution. A corporation can have its charter revoked at any time, putting an end to its existence as a legal entity. However, dissolution only occurs for corporations that request so or fail to meet annual filing requirements.

Fungibility The value of a corporation may be measured in terms of money and it may be traded in parts and pieces. Thus, members of a corporation (except for non-profit corporations) have a so-called residual interest. Should the corporation end its existence, the members are the last to receive its assets, following creditors and others with interests in the corporation. In addition, shareholders receive the benefit of limited liability regulations, making shareholders liable only for the amount they contributed.

Government may wish to employ the incorporated firm for governance purposes using the rules of equity: (1) it is the residual-claimant to the firm earning and asset-liquidation; (2) it contracts for the length of time of the firm; (3) it puts up a board of directors that hires the management team, monitors the chief managers, can demand audits for the firm, is informed about firm performance continuously, and participates in major investment decisions or operating proposals. When government moves the provision of public services to the incorporated firm, then it needs to consider that alternative governance structures result in different outcomes (Williamson, 1996).

There are two kinds of corporate governance forms in the world. First, control of the corporation is determined by a board of directors, which is technically elected by the shareholders. In practice, with the exception of takeovers, the board members are determined by the previous board. Second, the control of the corporation is divided into two tiers with a supervisory board which elects a managing board. In co-determination schemes half of the supervisory board may consist of representatives of the employees.

The leaders – presidents and chief executive officers (CEOs) – are picked by the board to manage the corporation. Corporations should ideally be controlled by their shareholders, but they can also be controlled by creditors including banks. In reality, the CEOs tend to prevail. In return for lending money to the corporation, creditors can demand one or more seats on the board of directors. For example, in Germany and Japan, it is standard for banks to own shares in corporations whereas in, for instance, the United States and the United Kingdom, banks are prohibited from owning shares in external corporations.

Economic organization theory in the Coase or Williamson traditions has explained how the incorporated firm may attack certain key problems in running enterprises with teams of people. The institutions of the corporation contribute not only to managerial control but also to the capacity to raise risk capital, or venture capital. An incorporated firm providing public services is, like a bureaucracy, a hierarchy, but it may employ outsourcing to a much higher extent. Generating its revenue through sales of services, its profitability is transparent. It may raise capital and make investments in response to market signals. The incorporated firm, operating with the provision of public services, faces the classical internal problems in economic organization, viz: How are transaction costs reduced? How is asset-specific information handled to avoid employee opportunism? When the public enterprise is a huge player like in infrastructure, then incorporation calls for market structure policy, levelling the playing field and avoiding market dominance, i.e. deregulation.

Disadvantages

The main disadvantage of the public incorporated firm is the lack of control of government and the weak accountability of its managers to political assemblies. Since a public enterprise, run as a joint-stock company, is not merely an enterprise, of whichever kind, or similar to a private corporation, questions of control and accountability loom large. Because the public joint-stock company delivers public services, it remains within the ambit of politics. Especially when something goes wrong, the leadership of the company will be held accountable to various bodies in the state, which may not be happy with being told that corporate governance must have a large degree of autonomy.

Moreover, the public joint-stock company cannot merely focus upon business and the making of a profit. As the delivery of public services, also those that can be fully sold on a market, has more to it than economics aspects, the government as well as parliament will monitor these corporations closely in order to account for their political aspects in relation to the citizens. Thus, it is not helpful to enshrine these public enterprises with the same amount of discretion as ordinary private enterprises. Take, for instance, the public reaction when a train derails with considerable damage to life and property, or when an electricity installation, such as a nuclear power station, fails. Such failures immediately become political issues.

To sum up

Public enterprises used to be employed for political patronage as absorbers of unemployment. They often had an excess labour force that resulted in loss-making performance with a constant need for government to cover deficits. The institutional change from traditional trading department to joint-stock company has permitted more leeway for governments to demand an increase in the profitability of the company. Thus, it can instruct the managers in the joint-stock company to cut their losses, meaning they should start shedding excess labour. If things go well, government may even demand a dividend payment on its shares.

Yet, to deliver public services is never simply business as usual. Care has to be taken to make sure the problem of monopoly or oligopoly does not arise, which calls for public regulation. In addition, the quality of the service in question must be ascertained, which again invites regulation. One solution to these concerns about public services offered by joint-stock companies is to combine regionalism with regulation, as in the European Union, setting up a common market not only for private goods but also for public services.

The new regional or global markets for infrastructure

The evaluation of the consequences of neo-liberalism for the conduct of operations within the business part of the public sector is still on. The findings from the assessment literature are mixed. One may mention telecommunications as the most successful case of deregulation and incorporation with full privatisation in some countries too. The most disastrous consequences are perhaps to be found with the privatisation of British Rail and its rail-road tracks. Outcomes are mixed in electricity, gas and water. In general, incorporation has led to:

1   Increased firm efficiency: firm output is up while employment is down in numbers.
2   Increased market efficiency: total quantity produced is up as more producers have entered the market.
3   Competition is up: the deregulated market is now often regional or even global.
4   Prices have not always come down: most often the unit price is down as with, for instance, airline services. But prices in transport and electricity have increased, partly as a result of the rise in fuel costs.
5   Profits have skyrocketed for the incorporated firms: the key question is to whom do these economic gains belong – government or the public?

Each country conducting evaluations of the incorporation strategy has its peculiar results, reflecting historical legacy, path dependency of reforms and idiosyncratic policy decisions, like the speedy privatisation that took place during the Thatcher era. Yet, incorporation and deregulation has created its own landscape, characterised by huge public joint-stock companies in head-to-head competition with big private firms, acting at arm's length from the owner. All kinds of alliances appear to be feasible, if indeed they are legal, given national, regional or international regulatory regimes. Some would be inclined to argue that monopoly has been replaced by collusion and oligopolistic competition. Whether that is so or not, the distance between the citizen/consumer and the public joint-stock companies has never been as large as now. Cross-border strategies and alliances have made the public joint-stock company less of an asset for the people and more of a revenue source for highly paid managers.

The ownership question was never resolved in relation to the traditional public enterprise, as governments embarked upon the strategy of incorporation and market deregulation. Many legal and economic challenges emerging from the liberalisation process engaged by the European Community with respect to state monopolies had to be confronted. In the areas of telecommunications, postal services, energy and air and rail transport, most significant developments have taken place in these key industry sectors within a short period of time. Issues raised by liberalisation and privatisation include consumer protection and public service obligations as well as the creation of "strategic alliances" in the telecommunications and aviation sectors. A comparative and international law perspective covers the extent to which monopolies have been opened to competition in the United States. Liberalisation measures negotiated in the framework of the World Trade Organisation are especially relevant to the area of telecommunications.

Reducing risk and complexity: PPPs in infrastructure

With ever-increasing complexity in infrastructure, government has incentives to look beyond its public enterprises in order to find partners with whom to share the substantial risks involved in huge undertakings. Bringing in the private sector calls for changes in the financing and or payment for infrastructure projects. Private companies will offer so-called PPPs (public–private partnerships) only if they can achieve a certain level of profitability in these joint ventures. The advantages for government lie in access to most recently available technology as well as risk sharing, with the private sector putting up substantial parts of the capital investments.

Private sector finance, provided by private enterprises, may help with constructing and managing public infrastructure facilities in partnership with government. Examples from Australia, Canada, Continental Europe, Hong Kong and the UK come to mind. There is also a potential for public–private partnerships in developing countries and transition economies. Public–private partnerships are now of greater interest to economists, engineers, investment banks and government bodies.

Public–private partnerships have become increasingly popular around the world as a way of procuring and maintaining public sector infrastructure, in sectors such as (1) transportation: roads, bridges, tunnels, railways, ports, airports; (2) social infrastructure: hospitals, schools, prisons, social housing; (3) public utilities: water supply, waste water treatment, waste disposal, government offices and other accommodation; and (4) other specialised services: communications networks or defence equipment. When considering whether to adopt the PPP procurement route, and the specific application of this policy approach in PPP contracts, governments consult international practices. They offer an integrated approach to financing PPPs within a public policy framework, serving as an aide memoire for those developing PPP policies or negotiating PPPs.

When government turns to using PPPs for its massive responsibility for infrastructure, then it is better served by incorporated public enterprises than the traditional trading department. The public joint-stock company has more manoeuvre to engage in collaboration with large or small private enterprises – flexibility and efficiency will be enhanced. The incorporated form of an organisation makes it flexible, autonomous and efficient when it comes to business.

Thus, public–private partnership is a key issue in the construction industry, causing much concern among contractors, funders and facility managers. Risk management methods can help the complex process of managing procurement via such partnerships for hospitals, schools, waste management and housing (Grimsey and Lewis, 2007).

Privatisation: the management issues

While privatisation is an inherently contested political issue, it involves some serious management problems. Some countries have pursued the privatisation option in relation to their SOEs (State-Owned Enterprises). Thus, large enterprises within telecommunications, energy and water/waste have been sold out in some countries. The resort to privatisation reflects more political ideology – the state/market separation – than essential state management theory. However, once a government embarks upon a privatisation policy, it faces some real challenges (Megginson and Netter, 2001). The basic difficulty is getting the price right.

Privatisation may be said to be successful if government is paid the "true" value of its SOEs and if the future provision of public services is not endangered. The massive privatisation reforms following the neo-liberal paradigm of the 1980s and 1990s have been criticised from exactly these two points of view.

Privatisation relieves government of the operational responsibility for certain public services (the business sector paid fully by user fees), but the overall planning obligation still falls upon state management. Thus, government must see to it that these services are forthcoming, also when private firms fail. Privatisation increases the burden for public regulation, i.e. it moves the responsibility from public enterprises to regulatory agencies.

Conclusion

Public management today knows several techniques and harbours alternative forms of organisation. As a result of continuous public sector reform, public management employs both administrative law and private sector law to get services provided and have people organised. Incorporation as strategy has been employed for the entire business sector of government and, in addition, in many areas of the soft sector. Even when the provision of services is paid for through taxes, the various teams of people receiving government contracts may be set up as joint-stock companies.

The strategy of incorporation then adds to the complexity of public management, increasing the heterogeneity of governance structures. When combined with tendering/bidding or quangos, it makes accountability more ambiguous in the public sector. When combined with privatisation, it may heave off huge chunks of public services to the private sector. Yet, government will, at the end of the day, always sit with the responsibility for infrastructure. The public has a legitimate expectancy that services in, for instance, infrastructure will be forthcoming, whoever happens to be the owner of the firm. Thus, government must monitor the sector even if it does not deliver the services by itself.

Essential summary

1   Traditional public enterprises often constituted a large portion of a country's economy. They are now a thing of the past.
2   Transforming the public enterprises (European tradition) or the public utilities (as in the USA) has been a major occupation of public sector reform.
3   Incorporation and deregulation have been high on governments' agendas for some time, but also massive privatisations have occurred in a few countries.
4   The incorporated form of an organisation appears to be the most suitable one when government conducts business activities.
5   The deregulation wave has been followed by a reregulation process that is not in agreement with the teachings of the Chicago School of Economics. It is often complained that regulation has actually increased and become more complex.
6   Providing infrastructure to the population remains a chief task for all governments, also after privatisation, incorporation and deregulation. When public or semi-private joint-stock companies make a lot of profits, then the question of monopoly or oligopoly surfaces again.

Suggested readings

Akintoye, A., M. Beck and C. Hardcastle (eds) (2003) *Public–Private Partnerships: Managing Risks and Opportunities*. Oxford: WileyBlackwell.
Campbell, C.T. and M. Wouters (eds) (2000) *International Deregulation and Privatization*. Ardsley, NY: Transnational Publishers.

Coase, R., P.J. Buckley and J. Michie (eds) (1996) *Firms, Organizations and Contracts: A Reader in Industrial Organization*. Oxford: Oxford University Press.

Eliassen, K.A. and M. Sjovaag (eds) (1999) *European Telecommunications Liberalisation* with H. Ungerer (Foreword). London: Routledge.

Geradin, D. (1999) *The Liberalization of State Monopolies in the European Union and Beyond*. London: Kluwer Law International.

Grimsey, D. and M.K. Lewis (2007) *Public–Private Partnerships: The Worldwide Revolution in Infrastructure Provision and Project Finance*. Cheltenham: Edward Elgar.

Megginson, W.L. and J.M. Netter (2001) "From State to Market: A Survey of Empirical Studies on Privatization", *Journal of Economic Literature*, Vol. 39, No. 2: 321–389.

Ogus, A.I. (2004) *Regulation: Legal Form and Economic Theory*. Oxford: Hart Publishing.

Thynne, I. (1994) "The Incorporated Company as an Instrument of Government: A Quest for a Comparative Understanding", *Governance*, Vol. 7, No. 1: 59–82.

Tirole, J. (1988) *The Theory of Industrial Organization*. Cambridge, MA: The MIT Press.

Williamson, O.E. (1996) *The Mechanisms of Governance*. New York: Oxford University Press.

Yescombe, E.R. (2007) *Public–Private Partnerships: Principles of Policy and Finance*. Oxford: Butterworth-Heinemann.

Young, A. (2001) *The Politics of Regulation: Privatised Utilities in Britain*. Basingstoke: Palgrave Macmillan.

Web resources

http://en.wikipedia.org/wiki/Privatization (last accessed on 22/03/2009).

9 Principals and agents
Public regulation

Introduction

Public sector reform has broken up the image of a monolithic public sector, run in accordance with bureaucracy. Instead, various kinds of organisations are active at different levels of government. Contracting out has invited many private organisations to deliver public services. And incorporation has made many public organisations look more private. Finally, third sector organisations have shown great interest in bidding for public contracts. How is this multiplicity of agents to be monitored and held accountable?

Public regulation has always been a major concern in public management. It aims at controlling certain parameters of the delivery of services and goods, such as price, quantity and quality. Public regulation may target both public and private organisations. It may be linked with the auditing of books financially, but this is not necessary. It may also have a legal orientation as in the health care sector when patients can file complaints against cases of assumed malpractice. The dismantling of the monolithic public sector and its replacement with a very diverse set of operators, organisationally speaking, increased the need for public regulation and oversight drastically.

Public regulation may target either the delivery of public services or private sector activities. Typical of the last twenty years is that both forms of regulation have increased significantly. Why?

Traditional public regulation: entry

In traditional public regulation, the focus is set upon public enterprises or public utilities, attempting to arrive at a regime that achieves efficiency in allocation. Two questions were much discussed in this theory of entry regulation, meaning that government would license the firms delivering goods or services on the one hand but set their prices and quantities on the other hand. Basically, it involved a trade-off between entry restrictions, which were favourable for the firms, and price and quantity decisions, which were negative for the firms – at least in theory. The two questions were:

1 What is allocative efficiency in infrastructure?
2 How is this to be achieved given lumpy goods and sunk costs?

This is not the place to debate the alternative theories offering various answers to these two questions (Tirole, 1988). Traditional regulation is no longer that relevant, as entry regulation is no longer as popular with governments. Instead, governments have adopted the regulatory stance that entry should be as free as possible, in response to the deregulation theme. Once entry regulation is dropped, and competition is forthcoming among various contenders, the regulatory focus has shifted to product regulation. Its key question is:

> With much competition in supply among public and private competitors, how can product quality and safety be enhanced?

The introduction of quangos and policy networks made this question all the more relevant. Government did not simply accept the philosophy of public management that insisted upon service delivery at arm's length from it. It also introduced regulatory boards that would monitor public service delivery in an effort to increase transparency, accountability and responsibility.

New public regulation: products

Deregulation, liberalisation and privatisation have made traditional public regulation almost irrelevant. Entry regulation is not a goal anymore, as the focus is upon the levelling of the playing field in a national, regional or global context. Emphasising competition in supply, leading to both contracting out and contracting in, the provision of public services has become heterogeneous, meaning that there may be several service providers offering the service in competition. All forms of competition are conceivable: public versus private organisations, bureaux versus enterprises, organisations versus entrepreneurs, different regional or local governments, etc. The following questions then arise: how are certain minimum levels of the quality of service guaranteed? How are grievances expressed?

The new wave of public regulation has targeted product regulation in an effort to define what quantity and quality of public services the population may expect. In some countries the drive towards product regulation has resulted in considerable growth of regulatory boards as well as in their activities. Perhaps the UK, with its highly dispersed organisation for public service delivery, has experienced the most rapid growth of the regulatory state, although it was hoped that deregulation, when initiated, would reduce public regulation.

There is almost a *paradox of reregulation* in new forms of public service delivery: the more there is liberalisation, the more there will be regulation. It may be interpreted as a sign that competition is not enough to ensure that customers are satisfied. Thus, in the health care sector reregulation has occurred after deregulation. The same holds for infrastructure sectors such as water. With so much new regulation, or reregulation around, how is one to understand the variety of regulatory regimes?

Regulation and risk

The expansion of regulation and the increase in regulatory bodies in postmodern society has stimulated a debate about risk being the major cause of the growth of regulation. One may ask how come there is such a need for new regulation in countries with an advanced economy and strong legal system – i.e. well ordered societies in the concept suggested by Rawls?

Thus, there would be as great a need to certify the quality of public services as there would be a demand for product assurance in the private sector. As the public sector reforms increase supply and the number of suppliers of public services, the consumers would feel a growing need for some agency that monitors all the varieties of supply. This explains the paradox of deregulation leading to reregulation.

Two contrary theories of risk have been launched as an explanation for the growth of the regulatory state. First, there is the *objective* theory claiming that the real occurrence of risks has really increased sharply in the so-called *risk society*. The term was launched by German sociologist Ulrich Beck, targeting the role of the mass media in revealing risks. In the risk society, there is a systematic approach to hazards and insecurities induced by ongoing economic modernisation (Beck 1992). He opposes natural disasters with "manufactured risks" from the economy and society.

According to Beck, a variety of risks are constantly increasing in postmodern society, which thus becomes a risk society. Moreover, risks harbour a "boomerang effect" as individuals producing risks are also exposed to them. The risk society replaces the class (modern) society, as all people will, in the future, be exposed to increased risks of various kinds. Thus, the risk society will not have a favoured upper class and a disfavoured lower class, because the distribution of risk originates from knowledge as opposed to wealth. Risk exposure is fundamentally dependent on knowledge and access to information, which may or may not correlate to economic status.

Post-modern society has changed with the introduction of multiple risks. It is true that risks are distributed unevenly in a population. As risks influence quality of life, government has a responsibility to inform people about risks and counteract them. People will occupy social risk positions that depend upon both information about dangers and aversion to hazards. Beck states: "In some of their dimensions these follow the inequalities of class and strata positions, but they bring a fundamentally different distribution logic into play" (Beck 1992: 23).

It is obvious that natural disasters like an earthquake or a tsunami may have enormous negative effects on dense human populations. But a risk society in Beck's conception is predominantly concerned with manufactured risks. The difference between the two is the human agency operating in the production and mitigation of manufactured risks: climate change, global pollution, dissemination of viruses and infections, spread of toxic substances, etc. Because manufactured risks are the product of human activity, policy may matter in reducing risk exposure and risk magnitudes. The counter-theory, however, claims that it is the perception of risks that matters – a *subjective* theory of risk.

Risks are mainly subjective, reflecting the bias of the actor when classifying events into risks or opportunities. Various social groups have different risk perceptions. Thus, the rise of the regulatory government is less the outcome of the post-modern society itself, but more the result of culture. This is the position of Aaron Wildavsky in *Searching for Safety* (1988), who saw the regulatory state as intimately linked with the rise of radical egalitarianism as a culture (Wildavsky, 1991).

Since risks are handled differently from one government to another, the key issue must be the perception of risk. And the perception of risk depends upon values that either lead to under- or over-exaggeration of risk, i.e. to bias. Since various social groups have different risk assessments, risk and culture becomes indistinguishable. This line of argument is to be found among scholars applying cultural theory to state management, such as Hood *et al.* (2004). Thus, Wildavsky's subjective approach to risk assessment appears better-founded than an objective approach. Yet, it is undeniable that the countries of the world "manufacture" great risks, such as the global financial meltdown in 2008. Despite widespread knowledge about the risks in credit markets, players in the financial institutions managed to create a situation of immense risk exposure by overleveraging. The global impact of the credit crunch seems to be more in accordance with Beck's objective approach.

A key issue in the debate about risk – objective or subjective – is the status of the precautionary principle, which has been more and more accepted by various governments. Is it warranted by objective circumstances in the risk society? Or is its endorsement driven by ideology, i.e. a bias against the market economy and economic growth?

Styles of regulation

With so much regulation going on, one understands the ambition to sort it out, finding the similarities and differences in regulatory styles. Thus, it has been argued that the regulation by the European Union is different in method from American regulation. Whereas public regulation in, for instance, the European Union takes the form of direct interventions in markets, based upon an authoritative decision by the Commission, American regulation goes over the judicial systems, with courts handing down the final decision. This difference reflects alternative legal traditions, linked with civil law and common law. Public regulation in the US takes the form of anti-trust cases or offences against environmental legislation, to be handled in an adversarial manner before a court. In the EU, the authority to regulate rests with the commissioners, whose decisions may be challenged in the European Court of Justice (ECJ).

The growth in regulation has offset attempts to theorise the variety of regulatory regimes. One of the most profound attempts has been made by Hood *et al.* (2004), making an enquiry into the bewildering nature of British public regulation, covering several different products, areas or topics. It is true that many paradoxes occur in public regulation, sometimes underestimating and sometimes overestimating risks. Can a pattern be found behind all the paraphernalia of risk and regulation? Hood *et al.* believe so, drawing upon New Culture Theory, launched by *inter alia* Wildavsky. They construct a somewhat complex theoretical framework to account for the diverse nature of public regulation, comprising all kinds of state intervention in society.

One may speak of various styles of regulation, as countries or regional organisations employ different models. A key issue is the place of courts in regulatory systems. In some countries, the ordinary courts are the arbiters of presumed violations of economic rules, whereas in other regulatory systems the regulatory agency may itself directly impose a verdict and a fine upon a perpetrator.

Trust and autonomy in regulation

The diversity of public regulation is a well researched set of phenomena. Differences in regulation – amount, orientation, method – may be explained by means of country legacies or with reference to different social groups having various risk philosophies, or cultures. What, then, is the common core of all kinds of public regulations? A principal–agent framework would target the quid pro quo between government as principal and regulatory agencies as agents.

Kreps (1990) has suggested a simple model of trust that captures some essential features, such as opportunism and collusion. The general trust model looks as follows:

Table 9.1 The trust game

		Player 2	
		Trust	*No Trust*
Player 1	*Trust*	1, 1	–1, 2
	No Trust	0, 0	0, 0

The Pareto-optimal solution of the trust game is (1, 1), but the Nash equilibrium of the game is (0, 0), since Player 2 will always choose his undominated strategy of No Trust. If cooperative solutions are allowed, then efficient solutions may be forthcoming, meaning, any solution between 0 and 2 that sums to 2. Moreover, if replay is added to the one-shot game, then meta-strategies may allow for Pareto-optimal solutions.

The relevance of the trust game to public regulation is twofold:

1 Government may trust various public service providers, meaning it will not regulate them in detail. The risk is that the service providers respond with opportunism, meaning that they cheat more or less in the provision or in the charges of fees. Government will then put in place encompassing regulation.

2 Government may trust their regulatory bodies in doing a good job and putting in high effort. This means that regulatory agencies can work at arm's length from government, enjoying much autonomy. However, autonomy may be conducive to opportunism, meaning that the regulatory agency either over-regulates or under-regulates. The government responds by monitoring the regulatory agency or setting up a competing one.

The trust game occurs in all forms of public organisation where government trusts an agency to deliver a service, rendering to it both autonomy and remuneration. If government does not trust the agency, then it may resort to public regulation. However, in relation to the regulators the trust game resurfaces, meaning that regulation is no panacea.

The British regulatory state: a pathology?

Government regulation of the market economy and the private sector was given an economic rationale in the theory of public regulation, separating between entry regulation (economies of scale) and product regulation (quality). It was given a specific role besides other public sector functions like resource allocation (production of services) and income redistribution (social security).

The critique of entry regulation, which led to massive deregulation, did not undo the rationale for government regulation of vital sectors of the economy, such the stability of money, the soundness of the banking and financial system as well as the respect of private companies for their public obligations. It is a basic theorem in the literature of Law and Economics that markets cannot operate without the institutionalisation of a framework of rules, which require a set of guardians to police it. One may point at the massive effort at regulation within the European Union when it put in place the Single Market, with twenty commissioners engaging in market surveillance.

Yet, when regulatory policy is combined with a number of other public sector reforms, allocative or redistributive, there arises the risk of the so-called garbage can process. According to Pollitt, this is what occurred in the extensive and recurrent British public sector reforms. As public services were partly privatised, partly contractualised, government experienced a great need to safeguard quality, although it no longer controlled provision. The solution is the erection of a large number of regulatory bodies to oversee the provision of goods and services that were produced earlier through bureaucracies or trading departments. For some reason, this web of regulatory bodies got into a spin, characterised by constant changes and additions, seemingly without rationale.

What turned Britain into a laboratory of political innovation? One scholar has dared to challenge the prevailing view that the British government under Thatcher and Blair became more liberal or decentralising. Instead, Moran argues that the result is an interventionist state, colonising and dominating hitherto independent domains of civil society.

Rules and incentives: the limits of public regulation

By enforcing economic institutions, government helps to shape outcomes in economic life. Whether government has a strong tendency to identify and enforce the rules that are most efficient is a contested issue. Adherents of Law and Economics maintain that government participates in a kind of institutional evolution towards the promotion of the maximum transaction cost minimising rules. What should be pointed out here is that rules can never restrain human behaviour completely. Incentives matter crucially for economic outcomes.

In relation to the 2008 financial crisis, it is easy to blame the regulators. But the key responsibility falls upon the owners of the financial institutions, who were "sleeping". Only the principal has a fundamental interest in protecting the assets of banks and other financial firms. If they are not vigilant, then the probability of disaster is not negligible, whatever system of financial regulation governments put in place.

Conclusion

The increase in public regulation comes as a surprise, given the ambition to effect a general deregulation of the economy. It can only be explained as a rational response to the growing diversity of supply of public services. With so many different forms of delivery, the citizens would wish to have some quality control as well as access to redress.

Cultural theory has offered insights into the peculiar regulatory regimes in place in several countries. It is no doubt true that different attitudes to risk play a role, which may be linked with a *Weltanschaung*.

In addition, one would search for the logic of state management as regulation. One logic is that of regional or global regulation of a common market for goods and services, including some public services. It is spelled out in the theory of multi-level governance. Yet, the regulatory state faces the danger of excessive transaction costs, as things become more and more complicated. When the delivery of public services like, for instance, the payment of British pensions is outsourced to India, then the filing of a complaint may become a messy affair with a risk for citizens losing faith in the nation-state. As the trust game models the interaction between government and regulators, the latter may also engage in opportunism.

The basic problematic in public regulation is: *Quis custodiet ipsos custodes* (roughly translated as "Who will watch the watchmen?"). The 2008 financial crisis reminds one of how impossible it is to devise a foolproof regulatory framework. Many actors – central banks, rating agencies, ocean investors, the Securities and Exchange Commission (SEC) and the Federal Reserve Bank (FRB) as well as the Financial Industry Regulatory Authority (FINRA) or the Financial Services Authority (FSA) – were involved in monitoring and overseeing the global financial system, but no professional economist predicted the size of the calamity that struck banks and financial institutions.

Essential summary

1 The multiple roles of government in regulation have been emphasised recently in state management theory.
2 Public regulation used to target so-called entry regulation, but it is today, after the process of deregulation, more occupied with product regulation.
3 Public regulation may cover the private sector or the various public agencies, such as hospitals and health care or schools and institutions, i.e. education.
4 Public regulation has become a popular strategy after public sector reforms and the NPM revolution, resulting in reregulation of the post-Weberian agencies.

5   The central problem of regulation is of a principal–agent nature: how can government trust regulators to be both loyal to government objectives and efficient in their results? Does public oversight of the private sector really work?

Suggested Readings

Beck, U. (1992) *Risk Society: Towards a New Modernity*. New Delhi: Sage. (German *Risikogesellschaft* published in 1986.)

Black, J., M. Lodge and M. Thatcher (eds) (2005) *Regulatory Innovation: A Comparative Analysis*. Cheltenham: Edward Elgar.

Cooter, R. and T. Ulen (1999) *Law and Economics*. New York: Addison Wesley.

Ericson, R.V. and K. Haggerty (1997) *Policing the Risk Society*. Toronto: University of Toronto Press.

Gibbons, R. (2001) "Trust in Social Structures", in K.S. Cook (ed.) *Trust in Society*. New York: Russell Sage Foundations, 332–353.

Hood, C., H. Rothstein and R. Baldwin (2004) *The Government of Risk: Understanding Risk Regulation Regimes*. Oxford: Oxford University Press.

Jordana, J. and D. Levi-Faur (eds) (2005) *The Politics of Regulation: Institutions and Regulatory Reforms for the Age of Governance*. Cheltenham: Edward Elgar.

Kreps, D.M. (1990) "Corporate Culture and Economic Theory", in J.E. Alt and K.A. Shepsle (eds) *Perspectives on Positive Political Economy*. Cambridge: Cambridge University Press, 90–132.

Maor, M. (2007) "A Scientific Standard and an Agency's Legal Independence: Which of these Reputation Protection Mechanisms is Less Susceptible to Political Moves", *Public Administration*, Vol. 85, No. 4: 961–978.

Moran, M. (2007) *The British Regulatory State: High Modernism and Hyper-innovation*. Oxford: Oxford University Press.

Pollitt, C. (2007) "New Labour's Re-disorganisation", *Public Management Review*, Vol. 9, No. 4: 529–543.

Slovic, P. (2000) *The Perception of Risk*. London: Earthscan Publications.

Tirole, J. (1988) *The Theory of Industrial Organisation*. Cambridge, MA: The MIT Press.

Viscusi, V. and J.E. Harrington (2000) *Economics of Regulation and Antitrust*. Cambridge, MA: The MIT Press.

Wildavsky, A. (1991) *The Rise of Radical Egalitarianism*. Washington, DC: American University Press.

—— (1988) *Searching for Safety*. Edison, NJ: Transaction Publishers.

10 Multi-level governance

Bringing in the two regional dimensions

Introduction

There have recently been efforts to theorise what is called state management as multi-level governance. This literature on public management as multi-level gaming goes beyond the traditional focus in public administration upon deconcentration and decentralisation, entering the regional level as a key stage for public management. The theory of multi-level governance has been much inspired by the evolution of the European Union, involving several supranational or intergovernmental bodies. Multi-level governance includes relations between governing authorities at all levels – the neighbourhood, municipality, province, national state, and regional and global institutions. Governance implies that state management is not restricted to government actors and structures but includes interested groups, organisations and publics.

The concept of multi-level governance attempts to theorise major changes in the present roles and powers of nation states. The transfer of competences upwards, to supranational organisations, sideways to quasi-autonomous actors, and downwards to subnational authorities implies a transformation of the structure and capacity of national governments. Within this context of sharing of responsibilities and increased regionalisation, the concept of multi-level governance has emerged as a framework for understanding the dynamic inter-relationships between different levels of governance and government. The interaction of nation states with subnational and supranational organisations and the increasing fluidity of political power suggest the relevance to the state of theories of networks, but also a critique of hollowing out of the state. One aspect of the turn away from a state-centred approach to government is regionalism.

Regionalisation (internal) and regionalism (external)

If multi-level governance is understood as the exercise of state authority along the various relations among levels of government, then it changed over the last two decades. First, decentralisation has often made local and regional governments more powerful to formulate and deliver policy. Local and regional governments are increasingly active in influencing public policies, improving the competitiveness of the regional economy and the well-being of residents – *internal regionalisation*. The governance of such regional policies becomes more complex and more demanding, involving multiple actors – public but also private – and requiring a rethink about how central and subnational governments should collaborate (Keating, 2004).

Second, there is the trend towards regional blocks of states – *external regionalism*. A number of free trade areas, customs unions, common markets and monetary unions have been created since the Second World War. And these regional blocks are increasingly active in policy-making, leading in some cases to the erection of supranational bodies such as secretariats, commissions, central banks and supreme courts (Farrell *et al.*, 2005).

Yet, multi-level governance is more than regionalism, whether internal or external. It also comprises the emergence of public–private partnerships as well as the privatisation of the delivery of public services. Taken together, these changes combine to result in the transformation of government into governance.

Key elements in multi-level governance

Multi-level governance comprising "new" forms of governance is consti-tuted by three main dimensions or developments. First, the vertical dimen-sion comprises interactions between higher and lower levels of government, including external regional bodies such as the EU. Multi-level governance as internal regionalisation is a key theme in the governance of the national terri-tory and in the work on the development of urban and rural regions. Multi-level governance as external regionalism comprises the growing regulation of regional blocks of their member states, transforming national legislation and streamlining economic rules – the so-called Europeanisation process, for instance. Vertical organisation becomes multi-level governance, i.e. multi-level administration, and is a form of joint administration between management levels and also other players based on negotiations and agreements.

Second, multi-level governance surfaces not only in territorial manage-ment and in work on urban and rural regions, but it also crops up in horizon-tal networks between governments or in the form of so-called public and private partnerships. Horizontal partnerships emerge on the regional or local levels where governments coordinate their efforts in various so-called func-tional organisations, i.e. special delivery forms being responsible for one

specific function that is overlapping in the jurisdictions. Horizontal cooperation is seen as a means to improve the effectiveness of local public service
delivery.

Third, multi-level governance may include private providers of public
services, such as infrastructure. The Anglo-American conception of
"public–private partnerships" targets welfare tasks by introducing market
solutions in order to reform the public sector. The EU framework with
partnerships focuses upon multi-level administration with a stronger degree
of horizontal and vertical partnerships with private organisations. The EU
promotes multi-level governance as a condition for achieving support from
the structural funds and the Interreg programme in the form of regional
development projects.

Rejecting a state-centred approach to government, multi-level governance
suggests a contractual approach with *inter alia* the design of grants transferred from central to subnational levels of government and the variety of
agreements between municipalities and with civil society, i.e. the public–
private partnerships. What, then, is the logic of multi-level governance?

Theory and concept of multi-level governance

The growth of multi-level administration takes place within hybrid ruling
systems mixing hierarchy and market, where democracy, legitimacy and participation are central concerns (Bache and Flinders, 2004). It may be seen as
an answer to new conditions for public sector administration. Multi-level
administration changes the traditional hierarchical political and administrative systems. It is seen as desirable to have binding interaction between
hierarchy and market in order to further local and regional development.
One might say that multi-level governance is a new framework for the management of the post-bureaucratic public sector, as typical of multi-level
governance is bargaining, focussing on the contractual approach to service
delivery.

Traditional state management is slowly replaced to some extent by a system marked by public players that negotiate, make agreements and form partnerships with the private sector or civil society in order to promote
development goals. Thus, agreements are made between public players, with
private players and with the civil society in different types of networks, and
these agreements and contracts becoming the basis for ruling.

However, one may raise the objection against the multi-governance
framework that it is more a single concept that an elaborate theory. It nicely
closes the sharp dichotomy between the supranational approach and the
intergovernmental framework by suggesting a gradual linking up of various
governments. But it does not answer crucial questions about authority in

these new structures:

1   Does multi-governance add to the state or replace it entirely?
2   How is authority exercised in multi-level governance, as surely there must be obligation and control in such a structure?
3   What are the incentives of people participating in multi-level governance?

One may analyse multi-level governance as experiments with new and more advanced forms of decentralisation or deconcentration (Hooghe and Mark, 2003), or one may look upon it as the employment of alternative modes of coordination besides bureaucracy and authority.

Hooge's and Mark's framework

Two quite distinct approaches to decentralisation have been suggested on the basis of different concepts of governance: "Type I" and "Type II" respectively (Hooghe and Marks, 2001). "Type I" decentralisation would involve: (1) that subcentral jurisdictions are multipurpose; (2) that membership in these subcentral jurisdictions does not overlap; (3) a fixed number of levels of subcentral jurisdictions.

Type I decentralisation offers a firm and coherent structure. This simple system in several European countries involves a set of provincial authorities each with broad-ranging, identical powers and responsibilities; and clear non-overlapping responsibilities for a given territory and population. In most countries, there will also be one other level of territorial public authority relating to the provincial or regional level within the country. "Type II" decentralisation, on the other hand, would comprise: (1) task-specific jurisdictions; (2) overlapping memberships; (3) unlimited number of jurisdictional levels.

Type II decentralisation offers a flexible design. Contemporary cases are to be found in large US urban areas, in which responsibility for different functions and services – schooling, police, road transport, rail transport, bus services, hospitals, planning, electricity, gas, water, etc. – are divided among many different bodies, each organised in their own way, with different territorial boundaries, different numbers of sublevels etc. Type II systems look messy, but they may be well adapted to a complex environment.

In my view, the use of the terms "Type I" and "Type II" are unfortunate, since these words already have an entirely different, established meaning in statistics (*Type I error* and *Type II error*). It seems more pertinent to distinguish between *territorial* decentralisation and *functional* decentralisation. This is how decentralisation has been analysed in the so-called theory of fiscal federalism, which covers not only federal states but also unitary ones.

Fiscal federalism

The theory of fiscal federalism attempts to offer some general prescriptions about how to organise the delivery of public services on a territorial basis as well as a functional basis. They are supposed to be based upon a calculus of benefits and costs to individuals from alternative institutional arrangements: what kind of policy community – territorial or functional – would a utility maximising individual choose to set up? Let me follow the answers given by one of the main inventors of this theory, namely Oates (1999).

One could argue that the failure of fiscal federalism to explain decentralisation accounts for the interest in a new framework like multi-level governance, which in addition may encompass regional coordination mechanisms. The theory of fiscal federalism is derived from strong microfoundations like welfare economics but it has not delivered many correct predictions about macro structures like territorial or functional decentralisation. The difficulty is that it tries to account for politics by means of an exclusively economic framework – Tiebout voting with the feet as well as the theory of clubs – which delivers normative prescriptions about ideal solutions that are easily undone by public choice theory. In my view, the theory of fiscal federalism contains a contradiction between allocative efficiency and distributional justice as equality. Let me explain quickly what I mean.

Fiscal federalism argues that the foundation of the delivery distribution of public services is to be found with the individual benefits and costs. Since the preferences of people vary and the costs of production are different from one location to another, only a decentralised approach can deliver an efficient supply of public services (Pareto-optimal local public goods). This is the first principle of fiscal federalism, which is a restatement of Tiebout.

Now, the second principle of fiscal federalism states that public service delivery is confronted by so-called externalities (positive or negative) as well as free riding. In order to derive an optimal supply of public services or goods, these externalities must be internalised and free riding must be stopped. The units for the delivery of public goods or services will only be handing down an efficient supply if they include all benefits and get the members to pay all costs involved. Thus, the size and membership of regional or local jurisdictions can be calculated and decided in a rational manner with the following implications:

1 decentralisation: services or goods should be delivered as close to the jurisdiction as possible, all other things being equal;
2 spillovers: the borders of the jurisdiction delivering services or goods

must coincide with the spreading out of externalities;

3　race to the bottom: benefits or costs that may be fully internalised by a single person or company should be allocated by the central government equally over all jurisdictions.

One may employ these implications to suggest an optimal structure of jurisdiction for the delivery of public services or goods. It would be a highly heterogeneous one, taking into account the variety in preferences and environments. However, fiscal federalism offers a third principle that is completely at odds with the three implications listed above: differences in wealth and affluence among the various jurisdictions must be equalised as much as possible by the central government, using systems of grants to either strengthen the budgets of weak communities to elicit certain programmes that the jurisdiction could not afford by itself. This is the third principle in fiscal federalism, calling for fiscal equalisation among jurisdiction. What, now, is the relevance of the principle of fiscal decentralisation, allowing for the maximisation of variety among jurisdictions, when the massive use of grants serves the purpose of minimisation of variety?

The theory of fiscal federalism never worked as a set of hypotheses about the empirical allocation of competences among territorial units, not even for the United States. However, it contained one interesting implication for the theory of multi-level governance, namely:

functional decentralisation tends to be more efficient than territorial decentralisation.

Thus, its argument in favour of single function units as well as horizontal partnerships recurs in multi-level governance. One theory says that single function units should engage in territory wise competition.

Competing jurisdictions (Frey)

According to a model of jurisdiction conceptualised by Swiss economists Frey and Eichenberger, government operations would be separated into multiple organisations. Each jurisdiction is a separate political unit, and may, for example, levy taxes upon the individuals living there. Moreover, each jurisdiction would be functional, dealing with one matter only, such as education, policing or roads. Jurisdictions would be overlapping, since the individuals covered by one jurisdiction, providing a function, might be covered by multiple jurisdictions in respect to other functions. Yet, the chief idea in the theory of FOCJ (Functional Overlapping Competing Jurisdiction) is that of competition, as jurisdictions providing the same function would compete with one another (http://en.wikipedia.org/wiki/FOCJ).

For some functions, each individual may choose which FOCUS (i.e. a unit of government operations under FOCJ) will apply to them; however, if the function is territorially bound, each town votes to select its FOCUS. For example, an FOCJ nation may have three police forces, with each town voting as to which of the three shall provide its policing.

This is, in my view, a rather impractical idea, modelling public organisations providing regional or local services as private firms. Public organistion is linked with territoriality in public law, and there is no need to change that basic idea or principle. An authority, whether regional or local, has no business in the jurisdiction of another such authority. Moreover, authorities are not in action for the purpose of making a profit by selling services in any jurisdiction, wherever it might be. Of course, service providers in the public sector, organised for example as joint-stock companies, may wish to provide services for more than one jurisdiction. This happens more and more in health care where regional hospitals serve more jurisdictions than the one that owns the hospital.

EU regionalism: mixing domestic and international politics

The European Union is often interpreted as an example of multi-level governance. As a matter of fact, the study of the European Union has been characterised by two different phases with alternative perspectives. The first phase – intergovernmentalism – was dominated by studies from the field of international relations. In the second phase, supranational insights were added from national political fields of study, including the making and implementation of public policy. The shift has been away from treating the EU as an international organisation similar to others (e.g. NATO) towards seeing it as a unique regional organisation and different from other international organisations. Thus, in some areas of activity – the first *pillier* – the EU displays more properties reminiscent of national political systems than of international organisations.

The multi-level governance theory crosses the domains of domestic and international politics, showing the increasingly fading distinction between them in the context of European integration. The theory of multi-level governance belongs to the second phase. Multi-level governance characterises the changing relationships between actors situated at different territorial levels, both from the public and the private sectors. Multi-level governance was first developed from a study of EU policy and then applied to EU decision-making more generally. An early explanation referred to multi-level governance as "a system of continuous negotiation among nested governments at several territorial tiers" and described how "supranational, national, regional, and local governments are enmeshed in territorially overarching policy networks" (http://en.wikipedia.org/wiki/multi-level-governance). The core of the concept of multi-level governance underlines the frequent and complex interactions between governmental actors and non-state actors mobilised in cohesion policy-making and in EU policy more generally.

The multi-level governance theme raises new questions about the role, power and authority of states, as no other international cooperation mechanism is characterised by such far-reaching regional integration as the European Union. The European Union is a political system with a European layer: European Commission, European Council and European Parliament, as well as a national layer and a regional layer. These layers interact with each other in two ways: first, across different levels of government (vertical dimension) and second, with other relevant actors within the same level (horizontal dimension). The European Union displays a mixture of intergovernmental cooperation between sovereign states and far-reaching supranational integration, resulting in deep entanglement of the member states' national policy levels with the European policy level (Hix, 2005). Multi-level governance theory describes the European Union as a political system with interconnected institutions at multiple levels, having unique policy features. But the concept of multi-level governance is hardly applicable to regional or global organisations other than the EU, as these regional cooperation mechanisms are more similar to international organisations.

Now, the concept of *Europeanisation* has become popular with scholars looking at how the EU impacts the nation-states of Europe. Thus, it is based more upon a looking-down perspective than the traditional looking-up view in the debate among functionalists, supranationalists and intergovernmentalists. The concrete manifestation of Europeanisation is the new bulk of EU law (Craig and Burca, 2003). Knill's analysis (2001) suggests various administrative adjustments in the member states, substantiating this claim with a detailed account of the administrative impact of EU environmental policy in Britain and Germany.

Yet, I would raise a word of warning here as "Europeanisation" is too loose a concept, often employed in post-modernist discourse. Actually, it means two different things: (1) looking down, it refers to the impact of the EU institutions upon member country policies and administration; and (2) looking up, it stands for the increasing political and legal integration of member states in terms of a common set of institutions – political, economic and legal – at the regional level.

Quoting Ladrech (1994), "Europeanisation" has been defined on the lines of the first: "an incremental process reorienting the direction and shape of politics to the degree that EC political and economic dynamics become part of the organizational logic of national politics and policy-making" (Ladrech, 1994: 69).

A contested issue in the Europeanisation literature is to assess the strength of the EU impact upon member states. Ladrech suggested that although the reorientation of domestic organisational logics is a feature of Europeanisation, a full homogenisation of domestic practices across Europe will hardly occur in the near future. Instead, pre-existing domestic structures are likely to have an important mediating effect on "external" pressures. This is in accordance with the first definition cited earlier amounting to a "bottom-up" approach to understanding the effects of Europeanisation, focussing upon nation-specific adaptation.

The opaqueness typical of the Europenisation theme stems partly from a research dilemma: how does one identify and measure the impacts from the EU level onto domestic structures: *policy structures*, extending to changes in legal and administrative structures; and *system-wide domestic structures*, i.e. changes in the nation-state as a whole? Some scholars argue strongly in favour of path dependency, meaning that country-specific administrative legacies and policy styles mitigate the top-down impact.

However, in Cowles *et al.* (2001) "Europeanisation" is defined according to the second definition cited earlier, as:

> the emergence and development at the European level of distinct struc-tures of governance, that is, of political, legal, and social institutions associated with political problem solving that formalise interactions among the actors, and of policy networks specializing in the creation of authoritative European rules.
>
> (Cowles *et al.* 2001: 3)

One may, of course, start from this definition of Europenisation (2) and enquire into the "downward causation" of Europenisation (1), i.e. Cowles *et al.* (2001: 3). Another difficulty in this literature, which is mostly interpreta-tive and qualitative, is to identify criteria for strong or weak Europenisation in the second sense (2), which fluctuates with the changing fate of new inte-gration proposals, such as the aborted draft constitution.

One may mention that when looking at Great Britain, Bulmer and Burch interpreted "Europeanisation" as "the extent to which EC/EU requirements and policies have affected the determination of member states' policy agen-das and goals". This is in line with the first perseptive cited, namely "the extent to which EU practices, operating procedures and administrative val-ues have impinged on, and become embedded in, the administrative practices of member states" (Bulmer and Burch, 1998: 602). They argued that change, albeit strong, has been more or less wholly in keeping with British traditions

(Bulmer and Burch, 1998: 603) – the path dependency theme.

The EU as a set of regulatory mechanisms

Multi-level governance could, in principle, be about anything in the alloca-tive functions of state management. However, the EU is mainly a regulatory mechanism with some redistributive tasks added. It does not produce any-thing in terms of public services. The EU concentrates upon economic regu-lation in combination with economic support to regions and clients.

Economic regulation is necessary in relation to the creating and running of a single market. This explains the emergence of EU law as one of the major institutional innovations in Europe, including the famous approach of "mutual recognition" to break down country-specific regulations and enhance regional integration. Is there a limit to this more specific concept of multi-level governance as regional regulation? Take the 2008 proposal of EU intervention in financial markets regulation.

The EU proposals signal rejects the Anglo-Saxon light-touch regulatory approach that has dominated financial markets during the neo-liberal period – the Washington Consensus. The main aim is to curb "short-termism" in financial markets, improve accountability and responsibility, assess risk better and increase transparency. Hedge funds and private equity face relatively little direct regulation. The EU hopes that its proposals are backed globally, first by the G20 and then by the countries with emerging economies. The proposals include a mechanism for oversight of big banks that straddle many national markets as well as of the internal workings of banks, where procedures to limit risk have simply been neglected. They also argue for a code of conduct to curb financial incentives that lead to excessive risk taking.

It is true that the European Commission has the sole right to initiate pan-EU financial regulation. Yet, the new EU proposals give emerging countries more say in global financial forums and raise the accountability of credit rat-ing agencies, accounting rule-setters, banks and their top management. EU also calls for the expansion of the Financial Stability Forum, a body consist-ing of regulators, central bankers and finance ministry officials from the G7 and other major economies, as well as international financial institutions and supervisory groupings. But will multi-level regulation of financial markets really help much? There is already a lot of national and international regula-tion of financial institutions. The difficulty is that regulation does not always work. There are several EU regulatory schemes, operated by the Brussels commissioners. But they have not all resulted in favourable outcomes, comprehensively assessed.

Regional or global levels of governance

The politics of global governance including the scientific study of global climate change fits multi-level governance well. Earth system analysis, as developed by the natural sciences, is transferred to the analysis of institutions of global environmental change. Rather than one overarching supranational organisation, a system of "multi-level" institutions is advocated. Industrial self-regulation, of horizontal transfer of national policies, of regional integration, and of improved coordination between international environmental organisations, as well as basic principles for sustainable use of resources, may enhance the global governance of the environment.

The rise of regional coordination and the further strengthening of global coordination suggest that nation-states face increasing difficulties in internalising externalities between them. Somehow, many policy issues are no longer national or subnational, but have ramifications beyond the nation-state. Fiscal federalism would entail that decision-making should be moved upwards, to either regional blocks of states or to a truly multi-national solution globally. The same logic applies to local issues where externalities transcend the municipality. Thus, one arrives at the concept of multi-level governance, from the local village to the global village. The complexity that results from handling these interdependencies may be both territorial and functional. But how is multi-level governance exercised? Does it amount to a new way of governing, a set of post-modernist tools focussing more upon negotiation and consensus than authority and compliance?

Multi-level governance: more than delegation and off-loading?

Multi-level governance is not only a new description of how authority or public power is distributed across jurisdictions: supranational, national, regional and local, reflecting the delegation upwards and the decentralisation downwards. This theme also contains the idea that power has become replaced by negotiation among players participating in networks. Thus, there are both horizontal and vertical networks, including private sector players: firms, entrepreneurs, civil society and NGOs.

The concept of governance is intended to mark this shift from authority to bargaining. In a "bargaining society", it is bargaining skills that decide who will prevail, not the possession of state authority. It is true that government has become more complex due to upwards delegation and downwards decentralisation, but is it really correct to describe governance as negotiation?

When it comes to the EU, then it seems misleading to characterise all of its policy-making or decision-making as bargaining. It often results in law, meaning those rules that are enforced by EU authorities. The activities of the

Commission and the Court belong better under authority than under bargaining, although it is of course true that much of the legislation in the Council results from negotiation among the member governments. The decision rules of the EU provide the member states with ample opportunities for blocking much needed reforms to be implemented in the member countries – the joint decision trap with Scharpf. Yet, some of the EU bodies exercise authority and not merely bargaining skills.

Decentralisation is not the same as negotiation. When competences are moved downwards in the state hierarchy, then regional and local governments may decide to outsource the provision of the corresponding services, or erect a public–private partnership. However, the responsibility for the competence still rests with an authority. If several competences are transferred to regional or local governments, then the total outcome may be the unravelling or hollowing out of central government. But it is not the same as bargaining entering the driving seat in the state as a whole.

Regionalism as policy networks: ultimate vindication of Mr Rhodes?

If one marries the concept of policy networks from Chapter 6 with the notion of multi-level governance in this chapter, then one arrives at a model of the future society as networking between public and private actors at all levels from the local village to the regional institutions above the nation-state. This would indeed be Rhodes' world.

Rhodes launched his policy networks model (1981) early on, and it was subsequently applied to the study of the EU by several British scholars. According to the Rhodes model, a policy network is a set of resource-dependent organisations. First, networks display various types of dependencies: the constellation of interests; membership; vertical interdependence; horizontal interdependence; and the distribution of resources (Rhodes 1988: 77–78). Second, Rhodes identified five different types of networks ranging from highly integrated policy communities to loosely integrated issue relationships. Between these one finds professional networks, intergovernmental networks and producer networks respectively.

At one end of the continuum Rhodes placed the so-called policy communities, characterised by stability of relationships, continuity of a highly restrictive membership, vertical interdependence based on shared service delivery responsibilities and insulation from other networks and invariably, from the general public. They would have a high degree of vertical interdependence and limited horizontal articulation (Rhodes 1988: 78). At the other end of the continuum, Rhodes put the issue networks, distinguished by their large number of participants and limited degree of interdependence (Rhodes 1988: 78).

A central feature of the policy networks approach is the notion of power dependence. Organisations within networks are considered interdependent: each organisation is dependent on others for certain resources – financial, informational, political, organisational or constitutional-legal – and it is the extent to which an organisation controls and can mobilise these resources which determines its power in a given situation. These "resource dependencies" are the key variable in shaping policy outcomes. However, interdependence is "almost always asymmetrical" and in some cases it is possible to talk of "unilateral leadership" within networks (Rhodes 1986b: 5).

The policy networks approach could, of course, be extended to cover multi-level governance, as its emphasis is on policy implementation according to a bottom-up perspective: "a process of bargaining between conflicting interests. Policy does not 'fail' but is actually made in the course of negotiations between the (ostensible) implementers" (Rhodes 1986a: 14). There is nothing which limits a network in any way, as it may include governments at any level and also the business community and civil society.

But is there no coordination in these loose partnerships? The *core executive approach* had the answer to this objection: the heart of government should be seen not merely as the important formal institutions (government departments, the Prime Minister's Office, the Cabinet and related committees, etc.), but also as the networks that surround them. The relative influence of the core executive in a given situation is related to the extent to which it mobilises resources. The emphasis of the core executive approach is interdependencies between formal institutions and informal processes as well as on the need to disaggregate government. Central governments will mediate the pressures of Europeanisation through such core executives.

Formal institutional structures provide a framework of resource distribution within which actors operate, but do not determine policy outcomes. The effectiveness of actors is in large part dependent on "the tactics, choices and strategies they adopt in using their resources" (Smith, 1999: 5). Central government is no longer a monolith and within multi-level governance the concepts of cabinet government and prime ministerial power do not provide the tools to investigate the interdependence that is at the heart of government as an element in wider policy networks.

Conclusion

Multi-level governance theory offers few precise hypotheses about public management. It is similar to network theory in the sense that this approach is more a manner of talking or describing the world than a set of definitive beliefs explaining the phenomena. Negatively, it removes the last vestiges of state sovereignty from governance. Positively, it merely underlines inter-dependencies, vertically or horizontally.

Public management as multi-level governance takes on a more substantial connotation when it is placed explicitly within a regional context, such as the European Union. When there are strong supranational bodies or intergovern-mental mechanisms, then the talk about multi-level governance makes sense, especially when subnational levels of government are involved. Transferring multi-level governance from the regional to the global context, or equating it with any or all forms of decentralisation is less helpful.

Multi-level governance theory is amorphous, as it is far from clear what it is that it explains. On the one hand, it comes close to saying that all depends upon all, underlining the growing interdependencies in the internet and free communication society. On the other hand, it seems to imply that productivity in service delivery is enhanced through linking up vertically and horizontally.

When multi-level governance is linked with regional regulation, then this new approach makes much more sense. The emergence of European law has changed the way the national governments operate in Europe, as they face a common regulatory framework for the delivery of many services. This "Europeanisation" of the nation-state involves not merely a large body of similar rules but also the monitoring of state compliance by means of supra-national mechanisms. It is profoundly contested how far this process of Europeanisation has proceeded. It probably makes sense to talk about the "Europeanisation" of countries like Romania and Bulgaria, but the core EU countries tend to maintain several of their key state features (Hesse, 2007).

However, when multi-level governance is identified in any network at any level of government, then the concept merely stands for reciprocities. It is too vague to be employed in a new framework for analysing government after the unravelling of the (centralised) state, as it is the same as a network.

Essential summary

1   State management has important regional dimensions, one being the role of substate levels of government and another being the impact of intergovernmental mechanisms on the state.
2   This double regionalisation of the state, provincial and local govern-ments under the central government on the one hand, as well as regional integration above the state on the other, has stimulated a theory of multi-level governance with strong elements of network thinking.
3   Multi-level governance may be modelled as involving both hierarchical links and vertical ones, as comprising both public agencies or govern-ments and private firms or entrepreneurs.
4   The problematic here is that multi-level governance structures may

become so diffuse and encompassing that they cover almost any kind of interaction among actors. It suffers from the same vagueness as the network concept.

Suggested readings

Bache, I. and M. Flinders (eds) (2004) *Multilevel Governance.* Oxford: Oxford University Press.

Blakeney, A. and S.F. Borins (1998) *Political Management in Canada.* Toronto: University of Toronto Press.

Bulmer, S. and M. Burch (1998) "Organizing for Europe: Whitehall, the British State and the European Union", *Public Administration*, Vol. 76: 601–628.

Cowles, M., J. Caporaso and T. Risse (eds) (2001) *Transforming Europe: Europeanization and Domestic Change.* Ithaca and London: Cornell University Press.

Craig, P. and G. de Burca (2003) *EU Law.* Oxford: Oxford University Press.

Farrell, M., B. Hettne and L. van Langenhove (eds) (2005) *Global Politics of Regionalism.* London: Pluto.

Frey, B.S. and R. Eichenberger (1999) *The New Democratic Federalism for Europe – Functional, Overlapping and Competing Jurisdictions.* Cheltenham: Edward Elgar.

Hall, P.A. and D. Soskice (2001) *Varieties of Capitalism – The Institutional Foundations of Comparative Advantage.* Oxford: Oxford University Press.

Hartley, T. (2004) *European Union Law in a Global Context.* Cambridge: Cambridge University Press.

Hesse, J.J. (2007) "The Europeanisation of Governance: Comparative Government and Public Administration Revisited", in *University of Tokyo Journal of Law and Politics*, Vol. 4: 28–46.

Hix, S. (2005). *The Political System of the European Union.* Basingstoke: Palgrave Macmillan.

Hooghe, L. and G. Marks (2003) "Unravelling the Central State, But How? Types of Multi-level Governance", *American Political Science Review*, Vol. 97, No. 2: 233–243.

Hooghe, L. and G. Marks (2001) *Multi-level Governance and European Integration.* Lanham, MD: Rowman & Littlefield.

Keating, M. (ed.) (2004) *Regions and Regionalism in Europe.* Cheltenham: Edward Elgar.

Knill, C. (2001) *The Europeanisation of National Administrations: Patterns of Institutional Change and Persistence.* Cambridge: Cambridge University Press.

Ladrech, R. (1994) "Europeanization of Domestic Politics and Institutions: The Case of France", *Journal of Common Market Studies*, Vol. 32, No. 1: 69–88.

Oates, W.E. (1999) "An Essay on Fiscal Federalism", *Journal of Economic Literature*, Vol. 37, No. 3: 1120–1149.

Rhodes, R.A.W (1997) *Understanding Governance: Policy Networks, Governance and Accountability.* Buckingham: Open University Press.

—— (1988) *Beyond Westminster and Whitehall*. London: Unwin-Hyman.

—— (1986a) *The National World of Local Government*. London: Allen & Unwin.

—— (1986b) "'Power Dependence' Theories of Central–Local Relations: A Critical Assessment", in M.J. Goldsmith (ed.) *New Research in Central–Local Relations*. Aldershot: Gower, 1–36.

—— (1981): *Control and Power in Central–Local Relations*. Aldershot: Gower.

Sand, I. (1998) "Understanding the New Forms of Governance: Mutually Interdependent, Reflexive, Destabilised and Competing Institutions", *European Law Journal*, Vol. 4, No. 3: 271–293.

Smith, M.J. (1999) *The Core Executive.* Basingstoke: Macmillan.

Snyder, F. (ed.) (2000) *The Europeanisation of Law: The Legal Effects of European Integration*. European University Institute Law Department. Oxford and Portland, Oregon: Hart Publishing

Web resources

http://en.wikipedia.org/wiki/FOCJ (last accessed on 13/11/2008).

11 Managing social security
The insolvency problem

Introduction

Financially speaking, a large part of state management is about handling the social security system, its charges, contributions or taxes on the one hand and its payments or outlays on the other hand. The basic questions surrounding any social security system belong to the standard topics in public finance theory, a sub-discipline within public economics. Here I will only deal with the management issues and bypass the micro- or macro-economics topics that are at the core of the construction of any social security system.

The social security system handles big money, as it receives a large inflow of money to be turned around and distributed to the citizens. The total size of the social security system depends upon the type of regime a country adheres to. The welfare state would be the most costly to administer, whereas the laissez-faire regime would be the least expensive. Most countries with an advanced economy operate some form of social security system, while many Third World countries go along with absolute minimum payments, relying, in addition, upon charity.

Managing social security systems, whatever their size and complexity may be, presents entirely different problems than the management of public services. Gone is the problematic from the principal–agent perspective, namely, the relationship between effort, incentives and real outcomes. Instead, the crux of the matter is how to administer a system of payments-in and payments-out in such a manner that it is sustainable in the long run.

Rule-focussed management

The social security system is basically a fund where people have assembled rights over time through observing obligations. Whatever the size of the fund, whether it is one national fund or many local funds, it still holds that the transfer of money in and out is completely determined by the social legislation. Thus, transfer payments – pensions, sickness benefits, unemployment outlays, child allowances, etc. – are minutely regulated in law and accompanying regulations, which the employees of the fund(s) have to enforce. The income side of the fund is as regulated as the outlays, whatever form the payments take: taxes, charges, obligatory contributions, etc.

Managing a social security system is entirely focussed upon getting the information correct. Thus, each individual participating in the system must be identified and his/her basic income profile must be established correctly. As the rights to receive money from the fund are partly based upon life-long contributions, these must be recorded correctly. Citizenship usually carries with it some entitlements like, for instance, a basic pension. Thus, social security management needs to have continuously updated information about the country population and immigration as well as emigration.

One aspect of social security management is the quality of the information in the system as well as how rapidly it can detect any attempt at forgery. Strange stories circulate about accounts with no physical person, dead people continuing to receive money and extended families with fake members. Yet, social security management may draw upon the paraphernalia of modern information technology, using information from different systems. Cheating is probably not a major problem in social security.

Workfare: introducing effort and discretion into social security

The term "workfare" literally means "work-for-your-welfare", sometimes formulated as "welfare-for-work". The concept and policy of "workfare" stems from the US, where "welfare" is the term for "social assistance", the bottom safety net in American welfare policy. Workfare programmes in different countries have four characteristics (Deacon, 1997; Torfing, 1999; Hvinden, 1999). Workfare programmes actually oblige able-bodied recipients to deliver effort or work in return for their benefits, but this is on terms inferior to comparative work in the labour market. Thus they are essentially linked to the lowest tier of public income maintenance by the government.

A workfare system replaces the existing welfare system, in which payments are made unconditionally to all welfare recipients, by a mutual contract in which welfare payments are granted conditionally upon a service rendered in return by the recipient (Marshall, 1992; Titmuss, 1958; Solow, 1998). The contract stipulates an effort, which may be a job in the private sector, or alternatively in a public job creation company, operating like a selection mechanism. It would ensure that only truly needy persons actually obtain public transfers. "Workfare" requires recipients of social assistance to work or to enrol in educational or job training programmes as a quid pro quo.

Should they refuse, their entitlement to financial aid and related benefits can be reduced or eliminated. Some workfare programmes encourage employers to hire recipients by providing all or a portion of their salaries on a short term basis.

Workfare entails that individuals should not receive financial assistance from the state, unless they are prepared to work or to participate in programmes leading to employment. Such an assumption flows from a philosophy that sees individuals asking for financial assistance as requiring the discipline from the imposition of stringent regulations. The intent of workfare programmes is to reduce the number of individuals receiving social assistance by inducing them back into employment. Positively, workfare programmes provide the unemployed with training or education, thereby enhancing their ability to work and to become self-supporting citizens. Negatively, workfare collides with the idea of entitlements in a welfare state.

Workfare programmes may consist of education mainly at the high school level, jobs in community organisations and in the private industrial sector. In one scheme, the participants received approximately $100 above their welfare benefits, and since refusal resulted in a cut to benefits, there was considerable incentive to participate. Both community organisations and private firms received a subsidy and placements lasted between 6 and 12 months. The evaluations revealed that the gains were minimal: "Economic conditions today are such that the use of workfare programmes cannot halt the growth in the numbers of social assistance recipients and in the length of time they require social assistance" (Shragge and Deniger, 1997: 80). The evaluation of other works programmes paralleled these results. "What really takes place is a kind of shuffling of the deck for the unemployed."

Workfare provides community organisations and industries in the private sector with a supply of cheap labour. Community organisations typically struggle to obtain adequate resources, and industrial firms welcome the offer of subsidised labour. The announcement of workfare programmes provides governments with the opportunity to gain public support by announcing their intent to "get tough" on welfare recipients. Workfare fundamentally alters the balance of relationships between the state and its citizens. Rather than assuring all citizens that they have a right to financial assistance when they are out of work (*entitlements*), workfare insists that this right is available only through labour effort. Some argue that workfare should be replaced by policies that require the state and the corporate sector to provide employment and that provide choices to individuals who need social assistance. Thus, some individuals will choose training and educational programmes and their voluntary commitment argues that they will succeed in these programmes. Others may opt to remain at home to care for children or elderly relatives.

The concept of workfare blurs the separation between "duty" and "activation". Workfare seeks a "mutual obligation", meaning that the recipient must contribute something in return for the received benefits. It is true that failure to meet the conditions of eligibility specified by active labour market policies of the Scandinavian type may result in the loss of unemployment benefits. But there would still exist a basic level of social assistance to each and every one. Contrary to this situation, workfare represents an offer "you can't refuse" (Lødemel and Trickey, 2001). Thus, the well-known active labour market policies of Scandinavia involve more options for the recipient. These policies have less strict enforcement of the claimant's duties and higher benefit levels. Another example is Australia's "Work for the Dole" scheme in 1998 with the concept of a "mutual obligation". The workfare programmes lack training elements and options (Kildal, 2001).

After Clinton's Personal Responsibility and Work Opportunity Act of 1996, the number of workfare programmes exploded. This law limited state educational and training programmes, eliminated constraints on workfare programmes, and terminated benefits after two years. American dual welfare covers categories of non-working citizens left to "Welfare", which offers a number of means-tested programmes at low levels. The main recipient group is lone parents, mostly young black mothers, whose income support has been an issue since the introduction of American welfare benefits in 1935. The chief idea behind workfare – that generous and permissive welfare benefits are conducive to passivity and lack of personal responsibility – a "dependency culture" – received much support in the neo-liberal or neo-conservative period. Only Denmark reports mainly positive outcomes of workfare.

American workfare programmes targeted a heterogeneous group of non-working poor people. The US government never engaged in active labour market policy-making to combat unemployment, nor constructed an adequate welfare system to protect citizens' income (except for the elderly). Workfare was meant to be an answer to both moral and financial challenges, reinforcing the work ethic and reducing costs in welfare. The primary aim of American welfare policy has always been to reduce poverty. Yet, the multiplication of workfare programmes after Clinton's welfare reform, in combination with the increase in poverty even among hard working people during the 1990s, lent support to the accusation that workfare was more punishment than generosity in solidarity.

New Labour in the UK launched "Welfare to Work" as one key element of the third way, in an effort to decrease the so-called "dependency culture". Blair wanted to create so-called partnerships between public and private sectors, consisting of programmes catering to young unemployed people aged 18 to 24, the long-term unemployed aged 25 plus, lone parents and disabled people. These programmes offered four options: a six-month sub-sidised private-sector job, six months with a non-profit organisation, paid training or education (for those without basic qualifications), or work in a new "environment taskforce". There was no fifth option of remaining on benefit; the unemployed are sanctioned by losing their benefits.

Some prefer the term "new-style-workfare", which combines the recipients' obligation to work and the obligation on the part of the state to provide services, such as child care etc. (Nathan, 1993). "Learnfare" and "fair work-fare" are also terms that are gaining popularity.

Centralised or decentralised administration

The administration of social security displays all kinds of variations. Some countries have one giant bureaucracy that handles the entire system, while other countries rely upon a mixture of a central government bureau and regional or local bureaux. In addition, there may be functionally specific funds that handle the payments for certain occupational groups or sectors of employees. The institutional variation is large when it comes to designing and operating social security systems.

Key issues in the theory of social security involve how the system is to be funded as well as how much of the payments should be collective and individual, respectively. Thus, one has debated for quite some time the advantages and disadvantages of:

1 minimum versus comprehensive insurance
2 pay-as-you-go financing or actuarial funding
3 tax financing or individual charges
4 financial management policies.

All kinds of solutions to these problems (1–4) may be found in the different social security systems of the world (Lindbeck and Persson, 2003). If there is one optimal system, then perhaps that would be Swiss social security, which has never experienced any major difficulty. It is highly decentralised and actuarial in intent, yet quite comprehensive in its coverage of life opportunities.

The major problem in social security: solvency

The basic risk in social security is not efficiency, although workfare is an attempt to reduce moral hazard in some of these programmes, such as poverty relief and unemployment schemes. For social security as a whole, the main concern is whether revenues will be sufficient for outlays. The sustainability of social security is threatened by the *worsening dependency ratio*:

1 as more and more people get older and live longer, the part of the population that somehow supports the clients in social security becomes smaller in relation to the beneficiaries;
2 as fewer young people enter the labour market, the burden upon them in supporting, somehow, the clients of social security increases;
3 as the number of people outside of the labour markets increase – through social exclusion – the outlays in social security go up.

These seminal trends in the economy slowly strain the entire system, calling for more revenues and smaller outlays to maintain the balance.

Governments may avoid this dependency ratio trap by simply refusing to make social security too encompassing in terms of life opportunities. If a government concentrates upon distributing a minimum level support for pensioners, unemployed and sick or disabled people, then the insolvency risk is sharply reduced of course. However, such a strategy may only be feasible in Third World countries where resource scarcity restrains social security policy-making.

Governments may leave the more costly parts of social security to the market, allowing people to buy private insurance beyond the minimum protection level, afforded by the state. Thus, countries separate between first "pillier" and second "pillier", linking the latter strongly with individual contributions or simply handing it over to the market. Some governments have recently privatised part of social security in order to reduce the coming burden upon the state, given the evolving dependency ratio problematic. However, countries with comprehensive welfare states have electorates who are lukewarm about such privatisations of social security. When all risks are taken into account, then a majority of the voters in several countries prefer some form of state guaranteed system for social security.

The pension puzzle

Constructing and supporting a viable financial system for securing old age pensions is tricky. There is immense institutional variation in this form of state management around the world. And both kinds of change, reform and decay, occur over time to them.

The comparative analysis of public pension systems around the world may employ a few key distinctions:

1   defined contribution or defined benefit;
2   funded or unfunded; and
3   actuarial or non-actuarial pension systems.

In defined contribution systems, the contribution rate is fixed while the pay-ments vary. In a defined benefit system, the payment is either a fixed lump sum or an amount determined by the individual's previous earnings. The degree of funding covers an unfunded (pay-as-you-go) system where aggre-gate benefits are financed by a tax on currently working generations. In a fully funded system, benefits are financed by the return on previously accu-mulated pension funds. The term "actuarial" refers to the relation (link) between contributions and benefits at the individual level. Unfunded (pay-as-you-go) systems can be either completely non-actuarial or have strong actuarial elements – "quasi-actuarial". Funded systems can similarly be either completely non-actuarial or actuarial. Moreover, while some elements of real-world pension systems are defined-benefit, others are defined-contribution.

The political debate over the consequences of a pension system include work incentives (the actuarial/non-actuarial dimension), capital formation (the funded/unfunded dimension) and risk sharing (the defined-benefit/defined-contribution dimension). Recent pension reforms have leaned towards more of actuarialism, more of funding and less pay-as-you-go, and more of defined-benefits. When confronted by the growth in pension outlays, some governments have simply increased the retirement age.

In whatever way a pension system is set up, the running of it depends upon the economic development of the country in question. Thus, weak economic growth and an increasing dependency ratio spell difficulties for governments in maintaining the system. A problem is the sharing of risk in economic life. Some pension funds put the contributions into the stock market, which may lead to both *bonanza* as well as *calamity*.

Real-world pension systems incorporate four kinds of pensions: (1) basic pension, equal for everyone, i.e. a guaranteed pension, below which no no-one's payments will fall; (2) a supplementary, mandatory pension, related to previous contributions; (3) occupational pensions, often the result of collec-tive bargaining; and (4) voluntary, private pensions. Some countries like the Scandinavian ones operate pay-as-you-go systems, whereas a country like Switzerland has a solid funded system (Orzag and Stiglitz, 1999).

Distribution: basic state management tasks

Besides allocation of public services with the involved requirement of effi-ciency or effectiveness, governments face a series of challenges of delivering programmes that respond to the distributional concerns in their communities. These distributional tasks may actually become comprehensive and very costly, when state management is to cover a variety of insurance concerns in the population. Questions of allocative efficiency no doubt dominated during the most recent public sector reform period of some twenty years, reflecting the political ideology behind neo-liberalism, neo-conservatism, the NPM movement and the Washington Consensus. Yet, the sharp economic downturn in 2008 coupled with a severe global economic crisis has led to more attention to distributional matters. They include:

1   poverty relief, or basic social assistance for those left behind;
2   income maintenance to protect against illness, injury and unemployment;
3   protection of savings in banks: the lender of last resort task.

Distributional policy-making may be guided by political philosophy, such as the well-known minmax principle of Rawls – the difference rule – suggesting support for the European welfare state with its deep distributional commitments. However, other political philosophies like Friedman's utilitarianism or Nozick's libertarianism may propose other and lesser distributional tasks in state management.

Conclusion

Managing social security presents no principal–agent problematic, which, though, is endemic in public services provision. Whatever system a country has opted for, the basic problematic is the solvency of the system: will revenues be enough for paying the outlays in the future?

Governments can, of course, renege on their obligations, cheating as it were against their principal, the population. In that sense, principal–agent gaming also occurs in the social security system. Everywhere, social security systems are under pressure due to the declining dependency ratio: more and more people become clients of the system while fewer and fewer young people enter the labour market to bake the cake which is to be distributed in social security.

Suggested readings

Castro-Gutiérrez, A. (2001) "Principles and Practice of Social Security Reform", http://www.actuaries.org/EVENTS/Seminars/Brighton/presentations/castro.pdf (last accessed on 7/11/2008).
Deacon, A. (ed.) (1997) *From Welfare to Work: Lessons from America.* London: IEA Health and Welfare Unit.

Enjolras, B. and I. Lødemel (1999) "Activation of Social Protection in France and Norway: New Divergence in a Time of Convergence", MIRE *Comparing Social Welfare Systems in Nordic Europe and France.* Paris: Drees.

Europe's Demographic Future – Growing Regional Imbalances (2008) Berlin: The Berlin Institute for Population and Development.

Ferrera, M. and M. Rhodes (2000) "Recasting European Welfare States: An Introduction", *West European Politics.* Vol. 23, No. 2: 1–10.

Giddens, A. (1998) *The Third Way.* Cambridge: Polity Press.

Goul Andersen, J. (2000) "Welfare Crisis and Beyond. Danish Welfare Policies in the 1980s and 1990s", in S. Kuhnle (ed.) *Survival of the European Welfare State.* London: Routledge.

Gutmann, A. and D. Thompson (1996) *Democracy and Disagreement.* Cambridge, MA: Harvard University Press.

Hvinden, B. (1999) "Activation: A Nordic Perspective", in M. Heikkilä (ed.) *Linking Welfare and Work.* Dublin: European Foundation for the Improvement of Living and Working Conditions.

Kildal, N. (2001) "Workfare Tendencies in Scandinavian Welfare Policies", Geneva: International Labour Office, http://www.ilo.org/public/english/protection/ses/download/docs/workfare.pdf (last accessed on 1/12/2008).

Lindbeck, A. and M. Persson (2003) "The Gains from Pension Reform", *Journal of Economic Literature*, Vol. 41, No. 1: 74–112.

Lødemel, I. and H. Trickey (2000) *An Offer You Can't Refuse: Workfare in International Perspective.* Bristol: Policy Press.

Loftager, J. and P.K. Madsen (1997) "Denmark" in H. Compston (ed.) *The New Politics of Unemployment.* London: Routledge.

Marshall, T.H. (1950/1992) *Citizenship and Social Class.* London: Pluto Press.

Nathan, R. (1993) *Turning Promises into Performances.* New York: Columbia University Press.

Orzag, P. and J. Stiglitz (1999) *Rethinking Pension Reform: Ten Myths About Social Security Systems.* Washington, DC: The World Bank.

Sayeed, A. (1995) *Workfare: Does It Work? Is It Fair?* Montreal: The Institute for Research on Public Policy.

Shragge, E. and M.A. Deniger (1997) "Workfare in Quebec", in E. Shragge (ed.) *Workfare: Ideology for a New Underclass.* Toronto: Garamond Press.

Solow, R.M. (1998) *Work and Welfare.* Princeton, NJ: Princeton University Press.

Titmuss, R.M. (1958) *Essays on "The Welfare State".* London: Allen & Unwin.

Torfing, J. (1999) "Workfare with Welfare: Recent Reforms of the Danish Welfare State", *Journal of European Social Policy*, Vol. 9, No. 1: 5–28.

12 Politics and jurisprudence
Law and the state

Introduction

Law enters all forms of state management, both public administration and New Public Management. In formal organisation, questions are bound to arise about the division of competences, the responsibility of key officials and the accountability of agencies towards their clients. In New Public Management, the levelling of the playing field will be a major concern among service providers looking for contracts to be allocated in various competitive schemes.

In civil law countries, jurisprudence and public administration used to be closely connected, as the most important law of a country was its constitutional law, setting the stage for vast bulks of administrative law. Public organisation as well as public sector governance constitutes institutionalised phenomena, relying heavily upon rules and their enforcement. But rules are the same as norms, and jurisprudence is the science of norms, in any case of the legal ones. Can one then conclude, as dominant legal and political science scholar Hans Kelsen did, that law and the state coincide completely or perfectly?

The role of law within the organisation of public service delivery is, without any doubt, a large one, but it has hardly been given the interest that it deserves. Law impacts upon public services in several ways. Thus, it defines eligibility, it provides for avenues of complaint and possibilities of redress, it regulates quality and user fees, as well as hands down requirements to be met in the production of the services. Whereas public administration has dealt with the problematics of organising the delivery of public services at great length, it has not examined the legal ramifications of public organisation or public services much.

Given that the public sector operates under a rule of law restriction in well-ordered societies, it is important to theorise the relationship between law and politics in public administration and public management. The purpose of this chapter is to identify some of the key issues and discuss them by offering the contending standpoints.

Law and Economics, legal positivism and pragmatism

Richard Posner has given the debate about the nature of law much recent stimulus, stating the case for a pragmatic approach underlining economic considerations behind law. It should, however, be balanced by an argument from politics, pinpointing the link between law and government through the concept of rule of law. Law is inconceivable as a mere pure system of norms, without a foundation in rule of law and its implications.

Recently, there has been a lot of interest in questions concerning the nature of law (Posner, 2004). On the one hand, moral philosophers have argued that law is close to morals and that judges will, whether they like it or not, be influenced by moral conceptions when they make legal rulings. On the other hand, economists counter-argue that law is pragmatic, orientated less towards high profile moral philosophy than towards the maximisation of utility for a society. Again, political scientists are a little bit late to enter the debate between philosophers and economists on topics that are of chief concern to them. The modern state is strongly linked with law (Kelsen, 2005). Public policies when transformed into public administration always take the form of the appearance of rules, to be enforced by a bureaucracy or agency in relation to the citizens.

I wish to argue here that the relationships between law and politics should be researched again. This is not an effort to revitalise a sharp distinction between public and private law, which is after all only valid in the Civil Law Family Tradition. Instead, I wish to argue that politics would not work without law, meaning that an understanding of the nature of law is crucial to theories of government. The Law and Economics school links jurisprudence with economics, pointing at the relevance of market considerations in the construction of contract law, especially in the deliberations about tort law (Posner, 1999). This position has been much debated, as judges and lawyers would be prone to pointing out that law is more about justice than utility. Thus, jurisprudence may be closer to political science than economics, and the link between law and government is rule of law.

One encounters rules and rule application in every sphere of the public sector. When there is a rule, then one may, of course, discuss its pros and cons, suggesting other rules that may replace it. This leads to the thorny question of the validity or efficacy of rules: which rules enter into the legal order, constituting valid law? The legal positivists argued that rules in the state are not merely moral norms, but have some additional quality that separates law from morality. One identification criterion could be policy-making, meaning that the rules had been laid down by government or the legislature. Another criterion of recognition could be court rulings, stating, for example, precedents (Hart, 1997). Finally, rules would be valid if they were somehow enforced, while moral norms seem to retain their validity even when they are not respected. The theory of the legal positivists has come under increasing criticism, as moral and political philosophy made more and more incursions into the area of law and jurisprudence (Barry, 1996). What, then, is a norm? And do norms exist, if so *how*?

The basic problematic: what is normativity?

The social sciences study social reality whatever it may consist of. Jurisprudence examines *normativity*, i.e. the meaning of norms and how they are to be interpreted and enforced in daily life. If political science, economics and sociology deal with *existence*, and jurisprudence with *duties* and *rights*, then how do these sciences relate to each other? Norms figure prominently in the social sciences, and jurisprudence studies what is valid law, i.e. actually existing legal norms. If this is so, then perhaps the difference between jurisprudence and the social sciences is only a matter of emphasis? Posner suggests that legal scholars and judges take more courses in the social sciences to improve themselves.

The problem of normativity may be formulated in the following manner, pointing at a paradox that Kelsen realised already in his "*habilitation*" from 1911 (*Main Problems in the Theory of Public Law* or *Hauptprobleme der Staatsrechtslehre*):

1   Norms exist in law and social systems, i.e. they are real.
2   Norms state what ought to be, aiming at changing reality.
3   Thus, norms do not belong to the actually existing reality.

The problem of normativity is then expressed as a conflict between ought and is with epistemological implications that are confusing. Thus, ontological and epistemological normativity may be separated:

Table 12.1 Ontological and epistemological normativity

		Ontology	
		Facts	*Norms*
Epistemology	Neutral	I	II
	Normative	III	IV

All four combinations are possible, which is conducive to confusion. Thus, it has been argued that positive economics belongs to combination I, explaining only facts, whereas normative economics would fall into category III, evaluating existing practices against normative criteria. Jurisprudence would, according to one school, fall into category II, analysing the norms that are given in, for example, the legal system of a country. Finally, there is position IV that jurisprudence is fully normative, both epistemologically and ontologically.

A definition of law

There is no established definition of the concept of law in the literature of jurisprudence. Instead, the disagreement about law is both large and of a fundamental nature (Posner, 1993). Some of the major positions in the philosophy of law include:

1   Law is a set of norms or imperatives.
2   Law is a set of decisions by judges.
3   Law is the behaviour of the legal machinery.
4   Law is the state.
5   Law is a set of moral principles.

The usual presentation of theories of law rests upon the distinctions between natural law, positivism, realism and pragmatism as well as the Marxist approach to law. Yet, the issues involved are so complex and multifarious that there are, in addition, different versions of these schools of law. Let me dare to suggest a definition that encompasses a variety of standpoints:

> Law is a system of decision-making by judges, enforced, with a high probability, by the state. These decisions are guided by norms, whether stated in statutes or argued by natural reason in cases, as well as practical considerations.

Dworkin's natural law approach underlines the relevance of moral philosophy – natural reason – to the decisions by the judges (Dworkin 1998). When there are so-called hard cases, the judges will consult moral theory in order to rule. Alas, moral philosophy is ambiguous, to say the least. Thus far, there is no coherent theory of morals to draw upon in order to decide legal cases, whether soft or hard. If one adheres to the ultimate values theory of morals, which I do, then one would be hesitant to invoke universal moral truths, as argued by, for instance, Max Weber (1949). Normativity is something that goes beyond reason, as reasonable people may disagree on what values and norms to pursue and respect in life. Yet, there is some scope of so-called natural norms and such like to keep promises, to tell the truth and to respect what belongs to others, paying compensation when there has been an infraction against someone, as argued by Hugo Grotius.

The positivist approach comes in several versions, two of which may be mentioned here: (a) Kelsen's pure theory of law as a system of norms; and (b) Hart's theory of recognition, covering both statutes and cases. They both focus upon the problem of identifying the norms that judges employ, given that natural reason does not suffice. All positivists agree that legal norms will, at the end of the day, be enforced ultimately through state sanctions. Norms that lack the force of institutions cannot be law, even if supported by moral principles. But which norms do the judges call the state to enforce when several norms are relevant or they collide (Posner, 1999)?

Kelsen is well-known for his theory of the basic norm as the marker that selects the norms to be applied. To him, legal validity is conferred upon norms through a logical process of deduction, which presents a model of law as a coherent body of norms at various levels of generality (Kelsen, 1967). Hart, on the other hand, claims that each national legal system has its set of identification criteria, which are laid down in what he calls the secondary norms. The distinction is between primary and secondary legal rules, where a primary rule governs conduct and a secondary rule allows for the creation, alteration or extinction of primary rules. However, the secondary rules are not to be seen as ordered in a hierarchical manner, or as completely coherent. They may include legislation in parliament but also judicial interpretation by judges in cases. Natural law scholars could not accept this approach, as legislation introducing *apartheid* could not really be law, even if enforced by the police (Kelsen, 1996).

Hart's different secondary rules force one to raise the question of whether one of them is more important than another (Hart, 1997). This is the issue of contention between adherents of statute law and protagonists of judge-made law, or between the civil law family and the common law tradition. For political scientists, analysing public policies, there can be little doubt that statute law plays an enormous role in the framing of policies. Yet, in American law the role of the judge in defining law is emphasised (Posner, 2005).

Yet, how can one be sure that Hart's primary norms are really enforced, or applied in the manner that the so-called legislator intended? The realist approach argues that law is the behaviour of the judges, i.e. regularities in how they tend to treat various cases. Thus, what matters is what actually happens in the implementation of rules, whatever the conception of the rules may have been among lawyers or citizens. Law is a gigantic machinery that only operates as the key players – the judges – behave. Somehow jurisprudence is not completely different from predictions in the social sciences, as there is no special legal validity. According to this approach, policy implementation and legal enforcement is basically of the same nature, namely, the taking of actions of bureaucrats. Legal validity is the same as the efficiency of law, according to Scandinavian realists such as Hägerström, Ross and Olivecrona.

Normativity collapses in this approach to law. Law is what the judges and public administration decide. In American realism, the scope of interpretation for the judge(s) is much larger than in Scandinavian realism. Interestingly, neither natural law nor legal positivists would accept the realist position, as it seems to do away with normativity completely. This raises the thorny issue of how validity and efficiency are related with regard to law.

From the realist point of view, these entities come down to be the same at the end of the day. But, is normativity then the same as reality? Recently, a fourth approach has emerged, namely, the pragmatist position. It is close to the realist tenet, but typical of legal pragmatism is the emphasis upon the practical considerations – utility – that the judge may bring to a case. When the law is applied, then it is not merely a matter of finding the correct norms and applying them. What is at stake is to find an application that maximises total or average utility for society at large. Thus, utilitarian considerations will enter into the deliberations of the judge, implicitly or explicitly. This was the famous Calabresi interpretation of certain cases in tort law, which Posner developed into a general theory of law as being close to economics. What could the judge fall back on besides utility when norms collide or no norms are available?

Given these four approaches to law, what are the lessons to be derived by looking at law from the perspective of politics? The basic questions that surround politics and law have been analysed by constitutional experts, Marxists and liberals. Given the strong process of judicialisation, we should raise them again and see whether we can resolve some of the riddles of law and politics. Let me begin such a reappraisal of classical themes by rejecting the theory which states that law and state are fundamentally identical.

The state = the law

This is the position of Kelsen (1966, 2005), stated early in his long career as a legal scholar with an acute interest in politics and public administration. The basis of this theory is the idea that both law and state depend upon enforcement, meaning, the use of sanctions. Thus, law is inconceivable without sanctions and it is the state that delivers these. Similarly, the state as machinery for the exercise of sanctions is impossible without norms that state when sanctions are appropriate and how they are to be applied.

I do not think that the nature of this identity can be resolved through conceptual analysis of "state" and "law". Much more is involved, especially for the political scientist. Taking an empirical approach, one may be interested in framing the problem in such a way that the question of this identity is an open one. Thus, one should, in principle, be able to make a number of enquiries into how the state supports, respects or undoes law.

Perhaps the suggested identity would be understandable if Kelsen had argued that the state tends to be a so-called *Rechtsstaat*, where government and administration would, with some high probability, achieve rule of law. Yet, with Kelsen's main or *pure* idea of law this is excluded, as the state to him is any state under public international law.

The identity between law and state is dubious for the following reasons:

1   Much state activity is not really covered by law: undercover operations, irregular activities, extra ordinary events, constant violations of rules in dictatorial countries.
2   Parts of law lie outside of the scope of the state, such as customs. They may be valid although the state is not called up to enforce them.

There is a basic hiatus between law and state that speaks against this conceptual identity. Law becomes outdated, but the state continues to operate *obsolete* rules. And state activities may be conducted without any legitimation in rules, such as the American invasion of Iraq. Questioning this Kelsen identity also makes it possible to conduct research into how different states support law, as it is well-known that that law enforcement in poor countries is much more problematic than in rich countries, for instance.

The state and the judges

When courts decide cases, then they bring support to the state by enforcing norms that the state has introduced. The basic idea is that impartiality in the courts strengthens the legitimacy of the state. However, it would seem strange to say that the judges have the ambition to reinforce the state. They are also supposed to apply the law against state officials who break the law.

Institutionalisation would be difficult without law. When policies have been decided and enacted, then they are transformed into programmes with rules to follow and a budget. Typically, the enactment of a policy focusses upon the objectives to be achieved as well as the chief means to be employed. The implementation stage involves the working out of the necessary tools for putting the policy into practice: law, instructions, budgets, etc. The judges play a critical role in making this institutionalisation possible. How?

Judges, whether in ordinary courts or in administrative courts, act as the guarantors of the legitimacy of the rules. Two important situations include, first, the punishment of wrongdoings under the rules and second, the possibility of testing which rules apply and how they apply. Given the importance of rules in social life, many countries employ a third type of surveillance, namely, the Ombudsman Office.

The role of the judge is somewhat different when it comes to breaking the rules on the one hand and making the rules more transparent on the other hand. Rule enforcement, being a probability phenomenon, cannot take too much disrespect for the rules. The judge plays a key role in sentencing those who do not abide by the rules, although judges are certainly not infallible. The police would face too much uncertainty if they were to enforce the rules themselves. Breaking the rules always implies two sides, the prosecutor or the litigator, arguing the case for being guilty and the defendant stating his/her case for innocence. The judge is given the role of final arbitrator.

Judges clarify rules and their application. It is a long way from the wording of a norm to its concrete application. One norm interacts with another, creating complexity. Judges are called upon to clarify the situation. Citizens need the option to test the rules in force, finding out which rules apply and how they are to be interpreted. The Ombudsman in its Danish version offers such a mechanism for rules-testing that any citizens can make use of. The Swedish Ombudsman, as representing the National Assembly, also has the right to initiate enquiries him/herself, besides being prosecutor.

Judges as politicians

Natural law scholars and realist as well as pragmatist jurisprudence underline the role of judges in defining what law is. They are the key players, although for different reasons. With natural law, it is the morals of the judges that decide the "difficult cases". In the realist school, law is the behaviour of the judges – end of story. The distinction between applying the law and making the law is often employed in relation to the behaviour of judges. Can it be maintained when the political system accepts legal review?

To natural law and pragmatist theories of law, it does not make a fundamental difference whether there is the competence of a court to test the constitutionality of a norm. The judge would, in any case, never apply a norm that goes against right reason or the maximisation of utility. For a legal positivist, on the contrary, the institution of legal review makes a critical difference, as the scope for judges to act increases considerably.

With legal review, the judges take on the role of being the prime protectors of the constitution and its underlying principles. They are not merely there to punish law breakers or interpret rules. They also shape the politics of a country by testing norms for constitutionality. When legal review becomes extensive, as in the United States, then the process of judicialisation of politics is enhanced. The Supreme Court becomes almost like a third chamber of Congress, with the competence to override both Houses.

Law will, under legal review, bring much to politics, testing policies on the basis of fundamental political principles. At the same time, politics will inspire jurisprudence, as there will be a need for thinking through the political premises upon which high profile cases are decided by judges.

The autonomy of law

When there is rule of law, then the courts are independent of government despite the fact that they are paid for through taxes. In a constitutional democracy, this independence of the judicial branch is given a high priority. Law will only be respected when it scores high on impartiality and neutrality.

The autonomy of law is less a support for the state in general than a contribution to one type of state, the *Rechtsstaat*. The political independence of judges restrains the exercise of state power. Law becomes a guardian of human rights. This aspect of law is only prominent with natural law scholars. Legal positivism contains both strands of thought, the Hobbesian *Machtstaat* and the Lockean conception of government as *trust*. In legal realism and legal pragmatism, it is not the protection of rights that constitutes a core concern, but utility or practical considerations about usefulness that are central.

The contribution of law towards the protection of rights has been neglected in several schools of jurisprudence, because they focussed too much upon the issue of the nature of rights in themselves. "Do rights exist?" was the classical question. The attempted solutions to this philosophical problem spanned a wide range of alternatives, from the position that rights are entity-like things to the position that they are merely a device of legal language without any independent reference.

Morality and normativity

Norms are given a major role in politics. Thus, Weber says that a political regime is always an order towards which actual behaviour is orientated, which may be considered legitimate or not. And neo-institutionalists emphasise the importance of the institutionalisation of norms for outcomes such as affluence and democracy. From where do these socially important norms receive their validity? This is the problem of normativity, which borders upon the general question of the validity of morality.

Jurisprudence, by clarifying which norms apply, offers a crucial contribution to the notion of rule of law in politics. If constitutional democracy is to be considered the superior regime invented by mankind, then the set of norms that distinguish it from other regimes need to be analysed. In a rule of law state, the norms must have a transparent form – this is the major contribution of jurisprudence to politics. However, how can the normativity of jurisprudence then be separated from morality in general?

Both natural law scholars and pragmatists argue that morality plays a major role in establishing law, whereas legal positivists and legal realists deny this, stating that judges should focus only on adjudicating law. The natural law school says that morals can give guidance to law, as there are basic principles that no one would reasonably reject, according to philosopher Scanlon (Barry, 1996). Legal pragmatists agree that jurisprudence will involve morals, but it is the matter of everyday moral considerations that have a practical import. In reality, judges decide more often by doing what is practical or useful to society than searching ultimately for what is right: *Fiat justitia, pereat mundus.*

Since morals offer a strongly contested discourse, where any agreement on abstract principles that could guide policy-making is absent, one can understand that the effort is to make a sharp separation between normativity and morality. Weber emphasised that when norms occur in social life, then they have to be analysed in an impartial and objective manner. From the standpoint of a Weberian theory of the social sciences, jurisprudence should not be told to relax its scientific standards and become indistinguishable from morals or normative economics.

High powered justice theory: Rawls against Posner

According to one basic argument in moral or political philosophy, jurisprudence when deliberating upon justice should be guided by natural law conceptions about what is reasonable or unreasonable in human society. Difficult questions about rights, due process and freedom versus equality can be penetrated and perhaps even resolved through examination of high powered principles of justice. These principles could give direction not only for law adjudication but also for policy-making. The adherents of this position – Rawls, Dworkin and Barry – all favour egalitarianism, favouring affirmative action and state redistribution of income and wealth.

The high powered principles argument can be criticised on two grounds. On the one hand, some people may suggest high powered principles other than egalitarianism, such as, for instance, libertarianism or utilitarianism. Thus, Buchanan has launched a highly conservative set of moral or political principles that would guide government and society. On the other hand, it may be argued, as Posner has done in several books, that law is not really based upon moral or political philosophy (Posner, 1993, 1999). Law is an autonomous fabric of norms displaying strong path dependency, mixing a variety of considerations such as fairness, economic efficiency, or utility, and politics in government policy. It involves trade-offs between alternative reasonable principles, resulting in tensions and incoherence (Posner, 2004).

The new institutionalism

A most basic concern behind law is the rule of law. Promoting rule of law forces the social sciences to theorise normativity and understand the links between political science and jurisprudence. The scope of rules is encompassing in all forms of public policies. Then, how is law related to government? Posner suggests that politicians and judges are of the same species (Posner, 2005). I doubt that very much. Law is more autonomous than Posner admits, but at the same time it is more linked with politics than with economic efficiency.

The new institutionalism in political science, sociology and economics underlines the role of institutions in shaping behaviour, especially in organisations. According to Johan P. Olsen, "institution" means both rules and norms on the one hand and practices and culture on the other hand. From the perspective of law, an institution is a rule that has a high probability of being enforced through sanctions of some sort, especially state sanctions. Changing the institutions of the public sector is a major concern in institutional design theory, which claims that outcomes depend critically upon which rules are enforced and how they are enforced.

Whether public services are delivered by means of bureaucracy or internal markets, all the players concerned would closely eye the institutions' governing interactions. Institutional transparency leads to good performance – this is the basic tenet in institutional design theory. From the legal perspective, what counts is both the quality of the institutions in place and their quick and predictable enforcement.

Bureaucracy or formal organisation makes use of law when protecting the bureau from arbitrariness on the part of the rulers or government as well as private invasion on the part of employees. The design of rules in a bureaucracy has a clear objective, namely, to reduce the risk of appropriation of public means for private benefits.

Similarly, the institutions of tendering/bidding and internal markets include strict rules about how tournaments and auctions are to be run in order to generate the best outcomes. In all forms of public procurement, there is a constant risk of institutional perversion leading to "*pot-de-vin*", kickbacks, commissions and straightforward bribes.

Conclusion

I venture to state that law offers a stronger protection of institutional integrity than customs and conventions, although sociological institutionalists would be inclined to disagree. If this is the case, then law carries a heavy burden in getting the institutions right in the public sector. However, legal scholars are in deep disagreement about the nature of law. Since the state appears in all variety of arguments about law, political scientists may perhaps bring some lessons about institutions, their evolution as well as design, to bear upon the standard philosophies of law, surveyed briefly earlier on.

Affirming the relevance of legal institutions for the structuring of the public sector, I would raise a warning against two extreme theories about the nature of law, namely:

1　State = Law, or the identity hypothesis. When governments act, then the legal situation is often characterised by opacity or ambiguity. Thus, it is far from clear which rules apply. It usually takes time before the application of norms becomes transparent and clear.
2　Law = Economic efficiency, the Law and Economics hypothesis. The use of legal institutions in public service delivery is seldom directly driven by the goal of maximising output and minimising, for instance, transaction costs. Instead, law as justice plays the major role, channelling public service towards an equitable supply to all groups in society on the same conditions, unless special treatment may be rationally motivated.

Law and jurisprudence participates in the institutional evolution in the public sector, either directly in the form of institutional design of new rules or indirectly through the judicial interpretation of already existing ones. It impacts upon policy implementation through the requirements of rule of law. And it gives direction for policy change by linking policy with moral philosophy, at least to some extent.

Law is ubiquitous and opaque at the same time. It pervades all social relations, but it is ambiguous. If this is the nature of law, then the legal pragmatists or legal realists have the upper hand in the controversy over the essence or jurisprudence. In the most recently formulated comprehensive theory of law, Richard Posner's, the seamless nature of law is strongly underlined. Yet, Posner draws the conclusion that this makes jurisprudence less scientific and more utilitarian or policy orientated. This entailment does not follow, because even if law is complex, incoherent and incomplete, it would still require specialist training to master it, meaning that jurisprudence is not only a craft but also an evolving scientific enterprise.

Essential summary

1   State management employs law as one of its most important tools for getting things done. Laws and regulations are essential parts of public administration and they can enter any form of private sector regulation.
2   One theory claims identity between law and state, making jurisprudence highly relevant for a theory of state management.
3   Reflecting on the nature of law brings several insights into institutions in general and public rules especially.
4   A theory of law based upon moral philosophy would underline the relevance of rights to state management in accordance with Hohfeld's typology.
5   The employment of law in state management appears to be much in agreement with a pragmatic approach to jurisprudence, underlying less high-strung moral philosophy but focussing more on the role of courts and tribunals in the actual operations of the working state.
6   Posner's emphasis upon utility instead of justice as the benchmark of law is not entirely without foundation, as there is often contradiction between norms that apply to a case. The judges may then rule on the basis of utilitarian considerations when perfectly valid norms collide. However, it is hardly the case that the maximisation of total or average utility directly trumps the considerations of justice.

Suggested readings

Barry, B. (1996) *Treatise on Social Justice: Justice as Impartiality Vol 2*. Oxford: Clarendon Press.
Dworkin, R. (1998) *Law's Empire*. London: Hart Publishing.
Golding, M.P. and W.A. Edmundson (eds) (2004) *The Blackwell Guide to the Philosophy of Law and Legal Theory*. Oxford: WileyBlackwell.
Hart, H.L.A. (1997) *The Concept of Law*. Oxford: Clarendon Press.
Kelsen, H. (2005) *Pure Theory of Law*. London: Lawbook Exchange.
——— (1996) *Theorié Générale des Norms*. Paris: Presses Universitaires de France.
——— (1967) *Reine Rectslehre*. Wien: Franz Deuticke.
——— (1966) *Allgemeine Staatslehre*. Bad Homburg: Verlag Dr Max Gehlen.
Posner, R.A. (2005) *Law, Pragmatism and Democracy*. Cambridge, MA: Harvard University Press.
——— (2004) *Frontiers of Legal Theory*. Cambridge, MA: Harvard University Press.
——— (1999) *The Problematics of Moral and Legal Theory*. Cambridge, MA: Harvard University Press.
——— (1993) *The Problems of Jurisprudence*. Cambridge, MA: Harvard University Press.
Rawls, J. (2001) *Justice as Fairness: A Restatement*. Cambridge, MA: Harvard University Press.
Weber, M. (1949) *The Methodology of the Social Sciences*. New York: Free Press.

13 Ecology and policy
How to combine the two?

Introduction

The state with all its organisation, resources and programmes is a set of man-made mechanisms, the limits of which are set by physics and biology. Thus, government must respect the implications of the natural sciences for the social sciences. Biology and physics (as well as chemistry) defines the degrees of freedom of human action. As the organisation of human activities display great variation, the implications of nature for the state are not highly restrictive. Yet, governments face increasing ecological demands in their policy-making.

The range of variation for the social systems of mankind has shrunk in proportion to the aggravation of the ecological problems of planet Earth. Thus, governments can no longer deny the policy relevance of global climate change and are forced to take the ecological consequences of social development into account to a much higher extent than before. As the energy–environment problematic unfolds during the twenty-first century, the degrees of freedom for governments are becoming less numerous.

Ecology and policy

More and more governments commit themselves to inserting an ecological dimension in their policy-making. No policy without an environmental impact assessment – this has become a basic meta-rule in policy-making. It is a late acknowledgement that human activities always result in an ecological imprint that can be more or less severe. It is a recognition that social systems perform within frames set by physics, chemistry and biology. In the early twenty-first century, this ecological awareness of the interaction between human systems and nature has never been so widely spread.

An environmental impact assessment (EIA) can be conducted for almost any environment component: air, water, ecological systems. It comprises an enquiry into regulations, baseline surveys, the impact predictions, relevant mitigation measures, the effectiveness of measures, as well as the limitations of the methods employed (http://en.wikipedia.org/wiki/Environmental_ impact_assessment).

An environmental impact assessment is an assessment of the possible impact – positive or negative – that a proposed project may have on the natural environment. The assessment would help ensure that decision-makers do consider environmental impacts when deciding whether to proceed with a project. The International Association for Impact Assessment (IAIA) has established what an environmental impact assessment amounts to, both identifying and mitigating the biophysical, social and other relevant effects of development projects prior to major decisions. Yet, it can be done in different ways, depending upon how risks are assessed – objectively as well as subjectively.

The ecology assessment refers to both inputs and outputs of the policy process. On the input side, nature provides raw materials for the production process that results in the provision of public services, such as energy, water, land and fresh air. Urban planning and the construction as well as the running of infrastructure requires enormous environmental resources. The availability as well as the price of these natural resources has to be entered into the policies and the policy-making process. The threat of depletion of vital necessities such as clean land, fresh water and fish looms large in more and more countries for governments to consider when making and implementing policy. It is not just a matter of physical planning or territorial management, as the ecological dimension makes itself heard in every policy.

On the output side of policy, it has been known since the advent of the industrial society and urbanisation that government must be responsible for certain critical services like the disposal of a variety of types of waste, the protection of fresh water resources and the maintenance or cleaning up of the landscape. How government can do this is a much-debated issue, as it need not rely upon bureaucracy but can contract with private providers for these services.

It is stated that richer is more ecological, meaning that the environment is better protected by a vast network of policies in the rich countries than in the poor countries. Somehow growing affluence spills over into a demand for a clean and healthy environment, lending support for ecological policy-making. In poor nations, such policies are often deemed as too expensive or impossible to fund. Some scholars have drawn the conclusion from this connection between affluence and ecological protection that economic growth does not present a challenge to the environment, but on the contrary supports a clean environment: the richer, the cleaner.

The paradox though is that pollution is closely tied up with the level of economic development. Thus, it is the rich countries that pollute the most, especially the large rich ones. It is when China and India start a strong economic growth process that they become one of main polluters of the planet. Thus, affluence does not only stimulate environmental protection but it also leads to pollution and larger environmental imprint.

Two ecological policy principles

Ecological policy-making can be done on the basis of two meta-principles that give different directions for the content and number of such policies. On the one hand, there is resilience, meaning, taking action *ex post* an environmental problem has arisen. On the other hand, there is the precautionary rule, which suggests that potential environmental dangers be removed immediately before they become real disasters. The debate between the adherents of the two guiding principles for environmental policy-making concern both models of human decision-making and conceptions of risk as well as strategies for blame. It is basically a question about engaging in environmental policy *ex post* or *ex ante*.

The idea of resilience is closely connected with the notion of bounded rationality. If human beings do not possess full information or clear-cut preference orders, then how can they correctly anticipate all kinds of environmental challenges or dangers? If complete rationality is impossible, then perhaps it is better to await disaster and then take proper counteraction.

The notion of precaution entails that one should not engage in any activity that leads to serious negative results. It is not enough to be rational after the damage is done. One should actively seek to prevent the occurrence of calamities. If one cannot predict them with certainty, then one can, at least, refrain from activities that could, with a certain probability, lead to negative outcomes.

Both these meta-principles for ecological policy-making are abstract, as they are general. The crucial question is what they imply when government is to make concrete decisions in various policy areas. The principle of resilience faces the difficulty that disasters may occur that are so huge that little can be done to improve the situation *ex post*. On the other hand, the idea of precaution faces the difficulty of specifying what the intolerable level of risk could be for various human projects. If interpreted narrowly, then eliminating all risks could mean removing all opportunities.

Which principle – resilience or precaution – is the one to be endorsed in a post-modern society aiming at maintaining economic growth while recognising the imperative of ecological considerations? The debate between cornucopians and environmentalists has been fierce, focussing upon the advantages or disadvantages of introducing one of these two principles as a meta-rule upon policy-making with an ecological dimension. This issue is rather complex, involving both empirical argument about the likelihood of catastrophes and conceptual or philosophical argument about the nature of risk and opportunity (Posner, 2006).

One contested theory claims that the perception of risk is at the core of the issue of resilience against precaution (Slovic, 2000). Moreover, this argument states in addition that these risk perceptions are culturally determined (Douglas and Wildavsky, 1983). This is not the place to sketch an overview of the arguments for and against New Culture Theory. Suffice it to mention that the politics of environmentalism involves to a certain extent not only factual assessments about dangers or pollution but also different evaluations of nature and how far human beings can be said to be allowed to exploit it, often in competition with other species. A radical version of the culture argument links the call for the ever-increasing ecological consideration in policy-making with the struggle over economic institutions, especially the status of capitalism (Wildavsky, 1997).

Ecological aspects of policies

For instance, the French government has decided that every new policy must have an environmental impact assessment attached to it. This is not to accept the precautionary principle, at least not in its most restrictive form, outlawing all measures that could be dangerous. This attempt to mix policy and ecology merely amounts to a call for an awareness about the environmental consequences of policy-making, either on the input or output side. It does not entail a commitment as to how any conflict between environmental protection and economic concerns is to be handled. After all, France plans a heavy expansion of its nuclear programme, albeit no solution to the nuclear waste problem is in sight.

Yet, having a meta-rule that calls for the continuous recognition of ecological aspects of policy-making is a major advance in comparison with the earlier pattern of policy-making, where environmental consequences were either neglected or consciously left out. One may ask whether the environmental assessment may be conducted in terms of more precise and perhaps quantitative criteria. Efforts have been made to come up with estimates of the environmental costs of policies, to be weighed against the more tangible economic benefits of the same policy. Such refined cost–benefit assessments may be complemented with estimates about the input of environmental resources into a policy.

It is widely known that environmental declaration and environmental outcomes are two different things. A government may well pronounce a new highly ambitious meta-rule to link ecology and policy. But it may be only talk, or strategy. When it comes to positing economic benefits against environmental costs, then a government may employ the free riding option, leaving environmental harm to be picked up by others, internally in the country, or externally.

The distinction between policy and implementation is highly relevant when understanding the difficulties in protecting the environment, within a country or internationally. In many Third World countries, there are numerous environmental laws and regulations, but they are not enforced. The well-known implementation gap or deficit within ecology and politics is driven by powerful forces: free riding, externalities, inefficient bureaucracies, weak enterprises, blackmailing, corruption, and merely fatalism or a culture of littering. The problematic of environmental policy-making – how externalities are to be internalised and by whom – has been much theorised in search of a practical but optimal solution.

The main types of pollution

Policies directed against pollution have developed rather quickly a set of policy tools. One may distinguish between small-scale pollution, such as littering, and medium-scale pollution, such as ozone smog, waste disposal and water purification, and finally global pollution, such as acid rain or greenhouse gases. Each of these requires its own proper policy technology.

To combat littering, which is a problem in poor countries, governments need to raise environmental awareness. Medium-scale pollution would require considerable resources in order to have large sites for secure waste disposal and proper installations for water purification. As they are lacking these resources, water and soil is often badly infected in poor countries which do not have adequate anti-pollution policies. When environmental awareness is lacking, together with limited resources for waste treatment, then the pollution from toxic wastes such as lead, mercury and arsenic may be lethal for whole communities. Finally, pollution becomes global when dangerous emissions travel large distances, either by air or by sea. To combat them, one needs international cooperation and trust.

Regional or international ecology presciptions

To overcome the temptation to engage in opportunistic behaviour on environmental issues, for instance, exporting the pollution to neighbouring countries, ecological considerations should be taken into account in policy-making and laws may be framed and accepted within a group of countries. Environmental standards are increasingly regional or international, depending upon whether they are recommended by a regional group of states (EU) or an international group of states (UN).

One may distil a set of policy principles that have backing in regional or international environmental planning:

- Pollution as negative externality: All forms of pollution must be identified and registered; however amorphous and widespread pollution may be, it must, in any case, be taken into account in the policy-making process. Bypassing of environmental harm potentially constitutes a crime, as forms of environmental impact must be stated publicly.
- Scarcity of environmental resources: Gone is the time when people thought there were plenty of environmental resources to be had. There is today a keen awareness about the processes of depletion and exhaustion in relation to all forms of environmental resources: energy, land, fresh water, fresh air, etc.
- Polluter pays: Environmental interference, in whatever form it takes, presents an externality to the community, whether it be local, regional or national. Thus, its costs must be picked up somehow. According to the dominant opinion, it is the polluter who should bear the costs of his/her pollution, with the implication that pollution charges are to be preferred ahead of taxes.
- Ecological balance or sustainability: Few people are deep ecologists denying entirely the right of humans to employ environmental resources for a variety of purposes, but most people would reject an aggressive anthropocentric stance that accepts any form of environmental intervention. The compromise between these two extremes is heralded in the idea of sustainability, but what it boils down to more concretely, for the making of policies and their implementation, is ambiguous.
- Market solution for pollution rights: The pollution charges should be set so that they reflect real costs of pollution or the value for people of not having pollution. It is believed that transforming pollution charges into pollution rights, to be bought or sold on markets, increases allocative efficiency.

The most well-known mechanism for a market solution to environmental policy-making is the carbon trading scheme, constructed on the basis of the Kyoto Agreement. Emission trading is emerging as a key instrument in the drive to reduce greenhouse gas emissions. The rationale behind emission trading is to ensure that the emission reductions take place where the cost of the reduction is lowest, thus lowering the overall costs of combating climate change.

The trading of emissions is particularly suited to the emissions of greenhouse gases, as they have the same effect on global climate change wherever they are emitted. The idea is to regulate total emissions by setting the overall cap, but companies would decide how and where the emission reductions will be achieved. By trading allowances, the overall emission reductions are achieved in the most cost-effective way possible. Companies are allocated allowances representing a tonne of the relevant emission, in this case carbon dioxide equivalent. Companies may emit in excess of their allocation of allowances by purchasing allowances from the market or paying fines. Thus, a company that emits less than its allowance can sell its surplus allowances. The total environmental impact is not affected, because the amount of allowances allocated is fixed.

Pigou or Coase

Public policy in relation to the environment struggles with the problem of finding mechanisms that imitate market solutions to the allocation of pollution items, satisfying the Coase theorem. The standard Pigovian approach to environmental taxation is considered outdated, as it may not estimate the costs correctly or have the taxes covering these costs. In addition, environmental taxes can easily be transferred onto the consumers, if prices are not elastic. Instead, according to the so-called Coase theorem, a process of bargaining between the polluters and those polluted would always reveal the true costs of pollution or real value of having a clean environment. In whatever way pollution rights are allocated, the decentralised approach will find and implement the efficient level of pollution where the marginal cost of pollution to the polluted is covered by its marginal value to the polluter.

Much has been written about the theoretical aspects of the Coase theorem, but it has not really been put to any empirical tests on a larger scale. However, one can view the process of putting the Kyoto mechanism in place as a vindication or failure of the Coase theorem. Does carbon emissions trading really work? And does it reduce the greenhouse effect? Carbon emissions trading involves setting up and running both domestic and international markets for trading emission rights in relation to different *carbon abatement* costs.

Some environmental NGOs criticise carbon trading as a proliferation of the free market into public spaces and environmental policy-making. They connect carbon trading with failures in accounting and destructive projects upon local peoples and environments, favouring making reductions at the source of pollution and engaging in community-driven energy policies, meaning policy should replace the market mechanism. Emission trading only contributes to solve the overall pollution problem, when the total cap is restrictive, because groups that do not pollute may just sell their conservation to the highest bidder. Overall, reductions would need to come through central regulation, although some environmental groups have bought abatement credits and refused to sell them. If the mechanism issues too many emission credits, then the market for pollution rights will be too small. There is actually the practice of grandfathering, where polluters are given free allowances by governments, instead of being made to pay for them. Critics advocate the auctioning of the credits with the proceeds to be used for research and development of sustainable technology.

Economists who favour Pigou solutions instead of the Coase mechanism point out that: (1) Trading may be a more complicated means of achieving the same objective; (2) Permit prices may be unstable and therefore unpredictable; (3) Some cap and trade systems pass the quota rent to business though grandfathering (a certain number of credits are given away for free rather than auctioned); (4) Cap and trade systems could become the basis for international trade in the quota rent resulting in very large transfers across frontiers; (5) Cap and trade systems are seen to generate more corruption than a tax system; (6) The administration and legal costs of cap and trade systems are higher than with a tax; (7) A cap and trade system is seen to be impractical at the level of individual household emissions.

The evaluation of the Kyoto regime will no doubt be an intense topic for debate until a new treaty comes into force in 2012. Whether the Kyoto mechanism is flawed or not depends much upon how one views the original allocation of pollution rights – which is what the Coase theorem basically rules out. Since China and India are not part of the regime and the US was allocated a small size of the pollution rights, one is not surprised that the Kyoto regime for environmental policy-making through the market mechanism meets with criticism, not only from the environmental corner (Hohne, 2006).

Conclusion

The coming together of ecology and policy is the new marriage, as policy-makers and environmentalists search for ways to insert ecological considerations, *ex ante* or *ex post*, into the policy cycle. Exactly how this is to be done will constitute a set of issues for the future. Environmental policy-making, just as policy-making with an environmental orientation, can be based upon alternative principles – what I called meta-rules earlier.

The rule of ecological sustainability may be seen as a compromise between two more extreme principles, crude anthropocentrism on the one hand and deep ecology on the other hand. However, it remains to elaborate what sustainability entails in detail as well as how it will be implemented by some design of a bureaucratic or market-like mechanism. Based upon the Kyoto Protocol, markets for emissions trading have emerged in several countries. However, the Kyoto regime is not yet a global one, as several important countries are not covered in its scope. The new regime, replacing Kyoto, must become much more restrictive and encompassing if the ambition to reduce the greenhouse gases is to meet with success.

Environmental policy-making has rapidly become a number one priority in several countries. But its technology is far from clear or certain, as administrative solutions compete with market-imitating ones. One thing though is crystal clear, namely, that ecology and policy will be closely married in the twenty-first century, in all countries – whether rich or poor.

Essential summary

1   Ecology is rapidly becoming a major aspect of state management.
2   The key to integrating ecology into policy-making and policy implementation is to be informed about the environmental inputs into policies as well as the environmental effects of policy.
3   A leading issue is the guiding principle to be employed in environmental policy-making: the rule of resilience against the principle of precaution.
4   Environmental policy-making has moved away from legislation and regulation as the policy tools, turning to the use of market-like incentives, such the polluter pays rule and emission rights trading.

Selected readings

Boardman, A., D. Greenberg, A. Vining and D. Weimer (2006) *Cost Benefit Analysis: Concepts and Practice.* New York: Prentice Hall.

Coleman, J. and S. Shapiro (eds) (2004) *The Oxford Handbook of Jurisprudence and Philosophy of Law.* Oxford: Oxford University Press.

Cooper, J. (2006) *Global Agricultural Policy Reform and Trade.* Cheltenham: Edward Elgar.

Cooter, R. and T. Ulen (2007) *Law and Economics.* New York: Pearson Education.

Douglas, M. and A. Wildavsky (1983) *Risk and Culture.* Berkeley: University of California Press.

Douma, W.T., L. Massai and M. Montini (eds) (2007) *The Kyoto Protocol and Beyond: Legal and Policy Challenges of Climate Change.* The Hague: Asser Press.

Glasson, J., R. Therivel and A. Chadwick (2005) *Introduction to Environmental Impact Assessment.* London: Taylor & Francis.

Hohne, N. (2006) *What Is Next After the Kyoto Protocol?: Assessment of Options for International Climate Policy Post 2012.* Amsterdam: Techne Press.

Light, A. and H. Rolston III (eds) (2002) *Environmental Ethics: An Anthology.* Oxford: WileyBlackwell.

Mishan, E.J. and E. Quah (2006) *Cost Benefit Analysis.* London: Routledge.

Morris, P. and R. Therivel (2001) *Methods of Environmental Impact Assessment.* London: Routledge.

Posner, R.A. (2006) *Catastrophe: Risk and Response*. Oxford: Oxford University Press.

Slovic, P. (2000) *The Perception of Risk*. London: Earthscan.

Stowell, D. (2004) *Climate Trading: Development of Kyoto Protocol Markets*. Basingstoke: Palgrave Macmillan.

Tietenberg, T. (2006) *Environmental Economics and Policy*. New York: Addison Wesley.

Vig, N.J. (ed.) (2005) *Environmental Policy: New Directions for the Twenty-first Century*. Washington, DC: CQ Press.

Wildavsky, A. (1997) *But Is It True?: A Citizen's Guide to Environmental Health and Safety Issues*. Cambridge, MA: Harvard University Press.

Web resources

http://en.wikipedia.org/wiki/Environmental_impact_assessment (last accessed on 13/10/2008).

http://en.wikipedia.org/wiki/Emissions_trading (last accessed on 22/03/2009).

14 The developmental state

From the Third World to the First World

Introduction

One may raise the question of whether the various frameworks for analysing governments from the output or outcome side have an inbuilt bias towards focussing upon the so-called "Western" state. Although it is true that much of the debate between the various schools introduced in the preceding chapters has examined the capitalist democracies, i.e. the countries that respect both the market economy and rule of law, attempts have also been made to model the Third World state.

In an interesting article, US budgetary expert Schick (1998) argued that NPM could not possibly fit a Third World country. When confronted with the choice between alternative institutional arrangements – bureaucracy and contracting out – Third World countries should opt for the traditional model of bureaucracy. Of course, the NPM regime would invite massive corruption in the handling of the contracts, before, during and after the contractual process. Yet, is this really a tenable argument? One can debate whether there is more than one model of NPM. Blair tried to identify a different version of NPM – *best value* – than that practised by the Thatcher and Major governments, linking it with civil society and public–private partnerships.

The basic choice in many Third World countries is not one between corrupt contracting out on the one hand and clean traditional public administration on the other hand. It is merely a choice involving two forms of corruption, one occurring in the tendering/bidding process and the other taking the form of an inefficient bureaucracy. Faced with a corrupt bureaucracy, it is difficult to understand why a Third World government could not attempt at least some modest forms of NPM. If successful, contracting out, or the setting up of executive agencies, may send signals to the traditional public organisation that they must correct their behaviour or face significant reductions.

Let us look briefly at some of the key models of public administration and public policy-making in the Third World, wherein the Third World state is linked with development in general, with economic growth in particular, with human rights and accountability as well as with clean government.

Development administration

When the former colonies began setting up their own states after the Second World War, then a discipline called "development administration" emerged as a speciality within public administration. The basic model in this sub-discipline was based upon an effort to link the new bureaucracies and levels of government with developmental objectives, such as rural development, urban management and poverty reduction. Development administration was strongly focussed on output and outcome, looking for efficiency in government more than legitimacy of procedures.

Development administration was taught within public administration schools or institutes, but the focus of the sub-discipline was really interdisciplinary. It looked at the civil servants and other government employees as involved in a giant effort at lifting the country out of poverty and tradition. It included the techniques of modern agriculture, the construction of million-inhabitant urban sites and the fight against tropical diseases. It paid too little attention to the problems of bureaucracies in the Third World, such as their lack of transparency and accountability.

To cut a long story short, one may say that successful development administration, moving a Third World country towards the First World, was reformulated in the model of the developmental state, whereas the less than successful Third World countries were approached as examples of anomalies in bureaucracy. The model of the developmental state – economic nationalism – provided the state with a strong role in promoting economic development. It was subsequently criticised as underestimating the contribution of society and markets to economic growth.

Economic nationalism

The model of the developmental state – government more or less guiding the process of economic growth – was only successful in South East Asia. Here, it is sometimes referred to as economic nationalism, to separate it from decentralised capitalism as well as the planned economy. Or one speaks of the "Singapore Model", given that Premier Lee Kuan Yew took the model to its extreme, transforming a poor Third World peninsula without hope to one of the richest and most dynamic countries of the world.

The model of the state as the promoter of stable economic growth, year in and year out, forcing the population to accept a high savings rate and channelling the surpluses into housing, health care and education, was never accepted or endorsed by Western economists. On the one hand, it was argued that the developmental state would be inclined to conduct industrial policies, especially of the import substitution type, which sooner or later would fail. On the other hand, market economists claimed that the Asian miracle came about despite the employment of the model of the developmental state. In Japan, South Korea, Taiwan, Singapore and Hong Kong, vibrant markets emerged that could raise and channel capital into productive investments. It was enough that government guaranteed the essential institutions of the market economy – contracts, free labour, *bourses*, joint-stock company form – in order that a peaceful and non-corrupt environment for business was put in place.

Economic nationalism failed in other continents – Latin America, Africa and South Asia – not necessarily because industrial policies proved inefficient, captured by special interests, but because the conditions of a vibrant market economy were not fulfilled. Under economic nationalism, government plays a major role in enhancing economic growth. If for some reason or other government fails, then it may spell disaster for the country.

Bureaucratic anomalies

The hope that the model of development administration raised about delivering large-scale positive results from government operations was soon turned into despair about the operations of bureaucracies in many Third World countries, especially in sub-Saharan Africa. Not only were government officials ignorant about how to promote rural or urban development, but signs of grave malfunctioning appeared some years after independence from colonial powers.

In the model of development administration, the civil servants and government employees are part of the solution, but in the various models of Third World state malfunction they become the villains, or part of the problem of lingering poverty and weak development. Government employs two kinds of people, administrative staff and professionals. The latter may certainly be most instrumental in raising the development prospects of a country, although the professionals tend to be recruited from outside of the institutes of public administration or schools of public policy. The models of malfunctioning in Third World states target the civil servants, or the chief bureaucracy at various levels of government.

Interestingly, several of the models of anomalies in certain Third World states already had names in the classical bureaucracy literature, especially by Max Weber. Far from believing that his ideal-type model corresponded to realities, Weber analysed how governments could drift far away from his ideal-type characteristics of an efficient and public interest-orientated bureau of civil servants. Thus, Weber observed the occurrence of "prebendalism" and "Satrapenherrschaft" in the process of forming modern states during the Medieval period, long before Third World scholars observed the same in the post-colonial state.

Once the critique of the post-colonial state was launched, there seemed to be no end in sight to uncovering the misdoings of Third World governments and their administrative apparatus. Thus, a variety of enquiries pinned down the "cleptocratic" state, the "criminalisation" of government and the occurrence of "sultanismus" or "patrimonialismus" with some of the former freedom fighters.

Good governance

The World Bank (WB) together with the International Monetary Fund (IMF) and the United Nations Development Programme (UNDP) has called for good governance in the Third World, partly as a reaction to disclosures of massive malfunctioning in state bureaucracies. The new emphasis of the WB and the IMF upon good governance can also be seen as a response to the critique against its earlier strategies for development. The key idea behind good governance is that the respect for human rights and rule of law would not only constitute a value intrinsically but also be useful extrinsically, as the economic regime that most effectively stimulates foreign direct investments and leads to stable economic growth.

The WB has adhered to different development strategies or theories of economic growth, depending upon which academic school recruited its key decision-makers. Up until the late 1970s, one may say that the Keynesians were more or less in the driving seat, suggesting massive governmental investments or the use of state regulation and planning. When planning failed to deliver, the WB turned around some 180 degrees and advocated free market economics in the form of the Washington Consensus, much influenced by the Chicago School of Economics (Serra and Stiglitz, 2008). Good governance, as the third major strategy of the WB, may be seen as a correction on the laissez-faire orientation typical of the Washington Consensus.

Good governance adds political and administrative objectives to the standard economic goals in growth and development theories. Consequently, the WB has funded a large research project to look into various aspects of the state, including its performance in terms of public administration, policy implementation and judicial predictability. This research strategy is in accordance with the new teachings from institutionalist schools in both economics and political science, underlining the positive implications of getting the institutions correct in a country. Economic and social development would result more from the unfettered operations of free markets and strong civil societies than from government intervention and regulation, as long as the "correct" institutions were in place.

The most ambitious attempt to measure the occurrence of good governance has been done in a WB project: "Worldwide Governance Indicators: 1996–2007" (http://www.govindicators.org). It actually divides good governance into two dimensions, although it employs six groups of indicators. Thus, on the one hand, "good governance" stands for democracy ("voice and accountability"), but on the other hand it also refers to state firmness: "absence of violence, government effectiveness, regulatory quality and control of corruption" (Kaufmann, 2003).

State management in several of the least developed countries of the world (LDCs) is focussed upon this second aspect of good governance in the WB, i.e. to reduce the occurrence of political violence and achieve a minimum level of government effectiveness, regulatory control and control of corruption. It should be pointed out that several countries score low on voice and accountability as well as rule of law but high on government effectiveness, regulatory control, control of corruption and absence of political violence, i.e. mainly the countries that have practised so-called economic nationalism with success.

One can debate whether democracy or state stability should be the first concern in some African, Caribbean and Pacific countries lacking good governance. I would be inclined to argue that removing anarchy and anomie would mean most to the population, which may require state firmness more than democracy. The problem is that in several of these countries strong government in the form of, for instance, military rule only triggers more instability, violence and protest. How can a minimum level of state management be achieved when society is in uproar and people lack basic trust in each other?

Rule by law or rule of law

As the process of globalisation rolls along, one may question whether the classification of governments into First World and Third World states makes any sense. One can certainly not deny that many governments do not operate well, especially in the set of the 50 poorest countries of the world. Yet, several Third World countries have closed the gap on the First World markedly.

The idea of good governance as a model of government harbours a contradiction between, on the one hand, democratic accountability, and on the other hand, government stability. In the WB major governance project, four out of the six indicators tapped the latter while two targeted the former. Numerous governments wish to increase rule by law in their states, but they reject the Western notions of rule of law such as separation of powers, federalism, party competition, judicial autonomy, constitutional review and a list of human rights as the ultimate benchmark of the evaluation of civil servants and government employees.

It is when states are no longer run according to rule by law that political stability becomes a chronic feature of public management. Not all Third World countries score low on rule by law, or government effectiveness. Some even score high, running countries with considerable wealth, such as the Gulf States. Whether countries that have reached state stability will somehow also develop into rule of law regimes is probably not to be taken for granted. Thus, governments may score high upon four of the WB governance indicators but low upon the other two, referring to democracy and judicial autonomy.

Conclusion

The framework for the analysis of state management should be flexible enough to contain concepts that cover the so-called Third World state. Actually, the sharp distinction between the First World and the Third World may have lost much of its relevance, as several countries that used to be poor have embarked upon a strong catch-up process. Government programmes everywhere may be inquired into for their contribution to social results, such as improved health, higher educational levels and fewer social problems. Public policies that improve rural and urban outcomes may certainly be devised.

Yet, the idea of development administration appears outdated. It smacks of planning and its rigidities as well as government mistakes. Public policies promoting economic and social development are not, first and foremost, an administrative task, as it involves the coordination of the efforts of people trained in different professions. A long-run process of development seems more likely to come about when a country offers a stable institutional framework, which allows for individuals to pursue their projects without impediments from bureaucrats. Micro management by public officials runs the risk of ossification, public programmes not responding to local exigencies or lacking flexibility. The WB in its governance project underlines both political stability and democracy as essential to institutional stability.

The search for good governance in the Third World is nothing other than an attempt to devise institutions in these countries that more fully restrain the opportunism of agents. The worst case scenario in a Third World country would be the simultaneous occurrence of weak social welfare or low national income and massive looting on the part of political and administrative elites, for example in Zimbabwe with Mugabe and Madagascar with Ratsiraka.

Essential summary

1 State management theory has focussed more on the so-called capitalist democracies, or the affluent countries with Western political culture.
2 Theorising state management in the Third World has resulted in a number of models: development administration, the developmental state, prebendalism and good governance.
3 The idea of good governance includes both democracy and rule of law on the one hand and effective state management or political stability on the other hand.

Suggested readings

Bayart, J.-F., S. Ellis and B. Hibou (1999) *Criminalisation of the State in Africa*. Oxford: James Currey.

Dwivedi, O.P. (1994) *Development Administration: From Underdevelopment to Sustainable Development*. Basingstoke: Palgrave Macmillan.

Farazmand, A. (ed.) (2001) *Administrative Reform in Developing Nations*. Westport, CT: Greenwood Press.

—— (ed.) (1991) *Handbook of Comparative and Development Public Administration*. Basel: Marcel Dekker.

Joseph, R. (ed.) (1998) *State, Conflict, and Democracy in Africa*. Boulder, CO: Lynne Rienner.

Kaufmann, D. (2003) "Rethinking Governance: Empirical Lessons Challenge Orthodoxy". http://www.worldbank.org/wbi/governance/pdf/rethink_gov_stanford.pdf (last accessed on 7/11/2008).

Schick, A. (1998) "Why Most Developing Countries Should Not Try New Zealand Reforms", *The World Bank Research Observer*, Vol. 13, No. 1: 1–9.

Serra, N. and J.E. Stiglitz (2008) *The Washington Consensus Reconsidered: Towards a New Global Governance*. Oxford: Oxford University Press.

Singh, R.S. (2006) *Rural Development Administration*. New Delhi, Bangalore: Anmol Publications.

Smith, B. (2007) *Good Governance and Development*. Basingstoke: Palgrave Macmillan.

WB Governance Project. http://info.worldbank.org/governance/wgi/index.asp (last accessed on 7/11/2008).

15 The comparative challenge
Are there different state models?

Introduction

State management may be conducted in different ways. One may speak of both pure types – public management as bureaucracy, as marketisation and as partnerships – as well as mixtures. Thus, universities rely much upon formal organisation whereas old age care often employs partnerships; the business sector has been transformed in accordance with market institutions favouring the buying and selling of services. Countries may rely upon certain standard operating procedures that enhance predictability in state management. Such country legacies may come up for reform when new models of public service delivery are diffused across the globe. Institutional change in state management is driven by the tension between state legacies on the one hand and new global models of public management on the other.

The NPM wave of reforms has, for instance, stimulated research into how far various countries have adopted the NPM philosophy (Bouckaert and Pollitt, 2004). It is a well-known fact that continental Europe has been much less enthusiastic about the idea of public management as marketisation than the Anglo-Saxon countries. Continental European countries either underline formal organisation (*Rechtsstaat*) or they employ partnerships in various forms. One may speculate whether there is some wisdom in state management traditions, meaning, that institutional change is path-dependent due to overarching reasons like predictability or efficiency.

The comparative study of state management may unravel how strong various national traditions tend to be. It may also uncover how alternative institutional forms contribute to outcomes. A key question is whether there is convergence or divergence in state management, meaning whether countries tend to adopt similar reforms as a result of global management trends.

Does every state have its style of state management?

In an interesting article, S. Kuhlmann asks what the driving forces were behind the major reform of the Paris city governance system. She offers a model comprising three factors:

1   Macroscopic: functional necessity or economic efficiency, meaning that the old bureaucratic system was no longer responsive to the changing needs of a metropolitan area.
2   Microscopic: a mix of strategy and tactics among the key participating political players.
3   History or legacy: path dependency meaning that the reforms were framed by French administrative tradition.

Rejecting hypothesis 1, she favours a mixture of tactical gaming by the choice participants and the Napoleonic legacy of centralisation and uniformity, this time focussing upon the mayor (elected by the city population) and not the prefect (appointed by the state) (Kuhlmann, 2006). Administrative reform always has to take into account the established system, but does this entail that there is always path dependency? In the case of Paris, the reform ended the historical *tutelle* of the French state over the city and introduced in one reform local government democracy.

Can one, then, say that each and every public sector reform is bound to display path dependency? Stating that all administrative reforms start from the status quo is, however, merely a triviality. The path dependency hypothesis becomes relevant and interesting only when it can point at some evidence that shows how a particular state tradition frames the future. And this was, of course, Kuhlmann's point, referring to the incredible influence that the prefectoral system has exercised over the French public sector since Napoleon created the system. But this raises another question: does every state have an administrative legacy?

State management models

Even if one admits the principle of path dependency, meaning that public sector reforms in each country are shaped by its past – cultural legacies, administrative traditions and history – one would not accept the hypotheses or assumption that each and every state has a peculiar state model. That would merely amount to a truism that states have a history, which is what path dependency covers.

The state models approach becomes much more challenging when one pins down the search of a variety of state models to a limited set. Here is a tentative proposal:

- federal state models such as the US, Switzerland and Germany;
- the American spoils system;
- the Westminster model (Whitehall);
- French unitary model;
- the old Soviet model;
- the Swedish "*ämbetsverk*" model;
- the colonial model(s);
- the New Zealand model (NPM);
- the *Rechtsstaat* model;
- the Arab state.

Although this list is entirely tentative and far from definitive, constructed by means of induction, it covers a good number of states. No ambitious attempt is made here to reduce these to a more parsimonious set of ideal-types, but one may speak of combinations with these models. Thus, Australia could be characterised as a mixture between federalism and New Public Management.

The New Zealand model (NPM)

Public sector reforms in New Zealand received lots of international attention due to the coherence and consistency of the policy to transform a welfare state into a market economy with public services delivered by contracting. They were conceived by people with a strong economist bent, focussing *inter alia* upon agency theory. There would be two contracts replacing tenure in the public service organisations.

First, there would be a round of tendering/bidding that would result in the awarding of contracts for a limited period of time, six years at most. Second, each employee would negotiate a performance contract that would specify in great detail what he/she was supposed to do during this period. Such a performance contract could run into hundreds of pages, because it would be the critical instrument in eventual legal battles over the possible non-fulfilment of the contract.

The New Zealand reforms were implemented with a firm hand, putting almost everything in the public sector on contract, with the exception of universities. Consequently, the number of public sector employees shrank, especially when the privatisation option was employed. Several public enterprises were incorporated and later sold off to the private sector. Social security was changed in a similar spirit. New Zealand became a private country in less than 10 years as a result of deregulation, downsizing, contracting out, incorporation and privatisation.

Yet, there was adverse selection in the new contracting regime that New Zealand embarked upon with such fervour. Thus, many court cases focussed upon whether the performance contract had been fulfilled or not. Transaction costs start climbing when contract law is used instead of administrative law for governance purposes. Recently, the governance has changed direction somewhat in New Zealand, underlining trust in long-term relations with service providers especially in old age care and social care (Chapman and Duncan, 2007). It is, however, premature to speak of a new NZ model.

Even when countries accept policy diffusion and take inspiration from public sector reforms in other countries like NZ, they may still come up with an indigenous policy mix of ideas, reforms and outcomes. Take the example of Malaysia (Dass and Abbott, 2008). Perhaps it was Premier Mahathir himself that rendered a major role to TQM (Total Quality Management) in the reforms of his government. Dawson (1994) lists six ingredients in TQM: (1) total management approach covering each and every employee; (2) continuous change by means of lean production plans; (3) quality control techniques of various kinds; (4) group problem solving techniques; (5) improving customer interaction; (6) promoting social capital at the workplace. In the NPM literature it has never been claimed that TQM was an absolutely essential part of public sector reform, especially since its components go back to rather trivial ideas. But in Malaysia TQM was vigorously combined with privatisation, contracting out and incorporation. However, a country like the Republic of South Africa (RSA) appears to have been more preoccupied with rightsizing its state management and correcting it against the threat of corruption than engaging in far-reaching reforms inspired by policy diffusion from abroad (Schwella, 2001).

Convergence in state management?

Recently, a few scholars such as, for instance, Pollitt and Kettl have suggested that state management in different countries is becoming more similar. The reason is the major reform trend created by the diffusion of the NPM philosophy (Bouckaert and Pollitt, 2004; Kettl, 2005). Yet, before one starts speaking of whether a country is now more or less NPM, one should keep in mind two important things concerning NPM, or perhaps better "NPM".

First, the New Public Management philosophy is hardly a coherent set of ideas that may be implemented in one and the same way. Instead, it is an amorphous outline of the public sector, comprising several different reform proposals that need not all be implemented. Thus, one country may endorse NPM in a very different manner from another country.

Second, the NPM philosophy arrived at the same time as many governments engaged in state modernisation. Thus, the two trends – NPM on the one hand and state modernisation on the other hand – may be confused. There may be many public sector reforms occurring, although they are not inspired by NPM. It is vital to distinguish between state modernisation in general and the NPM framework in particular, especially when one speaks of convergence.

In most advanced capitalist democracies, governments have engaged in state modernisation during the last twenty years. These reforms include: (1) deconcentration; (2) decentralisation; (3) performance measures: outputs and outcomes; (4) incentive strategies; and (5) deregulation and incorporation. This list of basic reforms to bring government up to date is different from the NPM reforms that cover: (A) privatisation; (B) contracting out and in: tendering/bidding; (C) executive agencies; and (D) public–private partnerships.

There are of course countries that carried out both lists of reforms: (1)–(4) and (A)–(D). But they are not numerous. Instead, one finds a divergence among countries, as some travelled the NPM road while others followed the state modernisation road. It has been suggested that a set of NPM countries – New Zealand, Australia, the UK and the Scandinavian countries – may be separated from Continental Europe that travelled mainly on the state modernisation road. This split would, according to this argument, be partly due to differences in legal traditions, i.e. the predominance of civil law within Continental Europe. It is more accurate to say that some countries went to exaggerations about the NPM philosophy whereas most countries employed some of its ideas in a modest and balanced manner (Halligan, 2004).

Generally speaking, the NPM philosophy does not offer a general model of public management towards which all countries may converge. It merely adds one more instrument for government to get the job done, namely, short-term contracting. There are two basically opposed evaluations of the NPM reforms.

Reinventing government (positive evaluation)

Osborne claims that his model of results-based government could render the citizens many of the outcomes they want, at a price they can afford. He even says that by attempting to identify and define the results citizens value, leaders could use competition – and customer choice – to save millions, while at the same time improving public services at all levels of government. True or realistic? Governments, both local and federal, are, according to Osborne, enduring their worst fiscal crises since World War II. But the political leaders, elected or appointed, continue trying to relieve the fiscal pain with accounting gimmicks, one-time fixes, spending cuts and tax and fee increases, to no avail.

In the 1990s, US public officials were promoting tax cuts and rebates. Today, the same leaders are announcing staggering shortfalls and cutbacks.

But big fiscal challenges always bring with them big opportunities. Osborne rejects the traditional medicine of raising taxes and cutting spending, and recommends innovations that have been pioneered to wring more bang out of the government buck. Osborne claims to provide a dozen concrete ways to do more with less: strategies that reduce spending while not undermining public services. But in reality he advocates an almost constant reduction in public budgets year in and year out (Osborne and Hutchinson, 2004).

Strategies in the *reinventing government philosophy* developed by Osborne recognise that voters seek a "third way", meaning neither big-government liberalism nor anti-government conservatism, but a fiscally moderate, non-bureaucratic but activist government. Strategic management is recommended by him as a tool for how those leading governments can define the future they want and then, hopefully, align public organisations towards creating that future. Osborne suggests "steering tools": community visioning, outcome goals, budgeting for outcomes as well as strategic evaluation, although their application has been questioned in organisational theory and public administration. I ask myself whether Osborne really helps leaders to new strategic management systems that invigorate the community's vision and goals and help government organisations target the achievement of them.

Hollowing out of the state (negative evaluation)

When the size of government is reduced due to the adoption of NPM policies, then a situation may arise that is referred to as "hollow state". The hollowing out of government entails that governments receive so little resources that it can no longer deliver adequately, especially in a long-run perspective involving the generation of new knowledge and innovations. Thus, a hollow state is not merely a government with reduced budgets and taxation, as it is also a matter of failing in the delivery of basic services as well as reduced capacity to innovate (Weller *et al.*, 1999; Fredrickson and Fredrickson, 2006). Hollowing out of the state occurs when the retrenchment of government is driven too far and cutback strategies hurt the supply of vital public services. How extensive, then, is the hollowing out of the state?

Suleiman (2003), favouring bureaucracy as the best overall institutional arrangement for government, makes an interesting comparative enquiry into the drive toward a civil service reform grounded in NPM philosophy. He argues that "government reinvention" has had unintended results, namely, limiting the bureaucracy's capacity to serve the public good. As bureaucracies have been under political pressure in recent years to reduce their size, there has occurred the unintended and often unrecognised outcome of growing deprofessionalism. Suleiman finds this evolution in both stable democratic societies and in countries consolidating democratic institutions more or less. His basic tenet is that the failure to acknowledge the positive role of an effective bureaucracy may slowly become a threat to democracy. Yet, it should be pointed out that when hollowing out occurs, the budget of government may not shrink, because former employees are re-employed under new contractual forms, such as with outsourcing. Is contracting out a feasible strategy and does it constitute an alternative to bureaucracy?

Comparative state management

Comparative studies in state management may serve two purposes. First, they may highlight critical changes in country models. By comparing two or more models of state management, one may arrive at a better insight into how a specific state model changes over time, becoming more similar or dissimilar to other models. Yet, one should not look upon every state as having a unique model of state management. Instead, one should try to limit the number of state models to a parsimonious set, comprising a set of ideal-types in the Weberian sense of concept formation.

Second, a comparative approach may be vital when examining the outcomes of public sector reforms. Thus, a change from one model to another is often said to be accompanied by a different set of outcomes, for instance NPM reforms increasing efficiency in service delivery. Comparative studies may help to determine how valid such model claims are by forcing the analyst to consider more cases, often within a different environment. Thus, comparative studies help the understanding of whether models of state management can be transferred from one country to another, as well as the limits of general organisational changes and their consequences.

The institutional changes that have occurred in the wake of the NPM revolution make it interesting to investigate the transformation of public service provision and, in the process, to include cross-country comparisons in order to understand similarities and differences. International trends like globalisation and economic integration have stimulated countries to make some common choices, but clear variations in receptivity, pace and types of change have also been found. Thus, the changes have demonstrated *path dependency*, or the existence of different paths depending on the historical, institutional, political and cultural contexts of each country.

Path dependency versus organisation model diffusion

Policy diffusion from one country to another is a well-known phenomenon. It has occurred with regard to the welfare state, in higher education reform and in insurance. What is now greatly discussed is whether the NPM philosophy is spreading to become a global reform movement. I doubt that because countries display not only path dependency but also different conceptions of state modernisation, some not favouring marketisation and privatisation which may be considered too neo-liberal devices.

The universal trend in state management reform is decentralisation, multi-level governance and networking. Recently, these reforms have targeted goals other than efficiency – inner or outer efficiency – like the enhancement of community goals such as social trust. The new efforts at regional organisations, such as the EU, may pull national organisation towards the ideal-type model of NPM, favouring liberalisation, deregulation and competition – "levelling the playing fields" in areas such as telecommunications, energy, water and transport – a few things that came about as a result of "Europeanisation".

It is true that countries watch what neighbours are doing when reforming their states. And diffusion may travel far, as when the Scandinavian countries started to adopt the NZ model. Yet, national legacies loom large in organisational model reforms. The US never adopted much of the NZ model, because lower-tier governments in the US had always employed much of contracting out and public procurement. For Continental Europe, path dependency is almost total, with Germany and France maintaining their historically embedded model of the *Rechtsstaat*.

Conclusion

It is true that governments in well-ordered societies decentralise the state and search for more of a post-bureaucratic organisation. However, it is not the case that all countries engage in agencification and marketisation. In one sense, most governments use tendering/bidding in their sizeable public procurement schemes. But is also holds true that several governments refrain from introducing internal markets or quangos. Some state models are more resistant to global policy diffusion concerning public sector reforms than others.

NPM is hardly a universal policy diffusion model for state management reform any longer. The two new major issues in state management are ecology on the one hand and regionalisation on the other hand. Governments are under pressure to insert ecology into each and every policy, but how can basic environmental principles be implemented in the agencies of government? Regional organisation is growing strong not only in the advanced EU. This forces governments to reflect on how state management is to be combined with the operations of regional organisations like the Association of Southeast Asian Nations (ASEAN), Caribbean Community (CARICOM) and the Union of South American Nations (UNASUR).

Essential summary

1   The marked differences between country models in state management have fascinated researchers for quite some time.
2   It seems that public sector reform is driven by waves of policy diffusion, affecting country institutions in various ways.
3   Some special country features of public administration have been analysed comparatively, such as the American spoils system, British Whitehall, the Swedish independent agencies, ministerial rule in Continental Europe and the Soviet model of party–state parallelism.
4   Some countries were highly receptive to the NPM philosophy, whereas other countries have been resistant to these reform ideas.
5   One distinguishes between the so-called NPM countries on the one hand and the so-called "Rechtsstaat" countries on the other hand. Yet, many countries have employed strategies like outsourcing, contracting in or out, incorporation and public–private partnerships.

Suggested reading

Bouckaert, G. and C. Pollitt (2004) *Public Management Reform: A Comparative Analysis*. Oxford: Oxford University Press.

Chapman, J. and G. Duncan (2007) "Is There Now a New 'New Zealand Model'?", *Public Management Review*, Vol. 9, No. 1: 1–26.

Dass, M. and K. Abbott (2008) "Modelling New Public Management in an Asian Context: Public Sector Reform in Malaysia", *Asia Pacific Journal of Public Administration*, Vol. 30, No. 1: 59–82

Dawson, P. (1994) "Total Quality Management" in J. Storey (ed.) *New Wave Management Strategies*. London: Paul Chapman.

Frederickson, D.G. and H.G. Frederickson (2006) *Measuring the Performance of the Hollow State*. Georgetown: Georgetown University Press.

Gregory, R. (2008) "Breaking Sharply with the Past: Government Employment in New Zealand", in H.-U. Derlien and B.G. Peters (eds) *The State at Work: Development and Structure of Public Service Systems in Comparison, Vol I*. London: Elgar.

Gregory, R. and L. Zsuzsanna (2007) "Accountability or Countability? Performance Measurement in the New Zealand Public Service, 1992–2002", *Australian Journal of Public Administration*, Vol. 66, No. 4: 468–484.

Halligan, J. (ed.) (2004) *Civil Service Systems in Anglo-American Countries*. Cheltenham: Edward Elgar.

Halligan, J. and G. Bouckaert (2008) *Managing Performance: International Comparisons*. London: Routledge.

Kettl, D.F. (2005) *The Global Public Management Revolution: A Report on the Transference of Governance*. Washington, DC: Brookings Institution.

Kim, P.S. (2008) "A Daunting Task in Asia: The Move for Transparency and

Accountability in the Asian Public Sector", *Public Management Review*, Vol. 10, No. 4: 527–537.

Kuhlmann, S. (2006) "Local Government Region between 'Exogenous' and 'Endogenous' Driving Forces: Institution Building in the City of Paris", *Public Management Review*, Vol. 8, No. 1: 67–86.

McCourt, W. (2008) "Public Management in Developing Countries: From Downsizing to Governance", *Public Management Review*, Vol. 10, No. 4: 467–479.

Osborne, D. and P. Hutchinson (2004) *The Price of Government: Getting the Results We Need in an Age of Permanent Fiscal Crisis*. New York: Basic Books.

Picard, L.A. (2005) *The State of the State: Institutional Transformation, Capacity and Political Change in South Africa*. Johannesburg: Wits University Press.

Pollitt, C., S. van Thiel, V.M.F. Homburg (eds) (2007) *The New Public Management in Europe: Adaptation and Alternatives*. Basingstoke: Palgrave Macmillan.

Pollitt, C. and C. Talbot (eds) (2004) *Unbundled Government: A Critical Analysis of the Global Trend to Agencies, Quangos and Contractualisation*. London: Routledge.

Saravia, E. and R.C. Gomes (2008) "Public Management in South America: What Happened in the Last Ten Years?", *Public Management Review*, Vol. 10, No. 4: 493–504.

Schwella, E. (2001) "Public Sector Policy in the New South Africa: A Critical Review", in *Public Performance & Management Review*, Vol. 24, No. 4: 367–388.

Suleiman, E.N. (2003) *Dismantling Democratic States*. Princeton: Princeton University Press.

Weller, P.M., H. Bakvis and R.A.W. Rhodes (eds) (1999) *The Hollow Crown: Countervailing Trends in Core Executives*. Basingstoke: Palgrave Macmillan.

Conclusion

State management: relevance of strategic management

Introduction

It is a long time since one divided society neatly into a public sector and a private sector, using concepts such as "state versus market", "bureaucracy versus private enterprise", and "plan versus competition". The public sector has grown and become diverse. It is linked much more with the private sector than before, as deregulation, incorporation and privatisation has led to a comprehensive levelling of the playing field.

The process of transformation of the public sector has been accompanied by the development of a number of theoretical approaches for the analysis of the public sector, from public administration over public policy and implementation to New Public Management. I suggest that "state management" be used as the general concept for the provision of public services.

Elements of state management

The purpose of a theory of state management must be to explain the delivery of public services, given the existence of a democratic political system operating in a vibrant market economy. A number of requirements may be stated in relation to public services, such as:

1 cost effectiveness
2 accessibility
3 equality
4 quality
5 quantity
6 environmental soundness.

A theory of state management would comprise an argument about how these evaluation criteria are to be met in terms of which mechanisms and under what forms. State management may be organised in several alternative ways:

1 formal organisation and hierarchy;
2 market relationships: tendering and bidding;
3 partnerships: networks, cooperation and trust.

A theory of state management would explain how these alternative mechanisms operate and how they contribute to performance according to the evaluation criteria cited earlier. Different types of public services may require certain institutions in order to operate efficiently.

Countries develop public sector legacies, favouring certain delivery mechanisms. General models of the public sector may, at times, change these country legacies, but there remains a strong dose of path dependency in the history of public service delivery.

State management is not the same as management. Although much can be learned from theories of management in general, and strategic management in particular, public management has its distinctive features due to the basic fact that it is state management. Politics cannot be separated from management when it comes to organising the delivery of public services. Let me spell this out in relation to the concept of strategic management in the public sector.

Meaning of strategic management in the public sector

After many years of public sector reforms in advanced capitalist democracies, a concept of strategic management for the delivery of public services would be highly relevant for the conduct of operations by public organisations, or bureaux, as well as in schemes of outsourcing. However, it must take into account the specific features of the public sector (such as the occurrence of bounded rationality and the risk of garbage can decision processes) as well as the implications of the rule of law. Outcome measures constitute the starting point in the derivation of public sector strategic management. As the "new public organisation" replaces bureaucracy, then the flat and boundaryless organisation will need more of a strategic management focus, especially when combined with outsourcing.

The concept of management originated in the private sector with respect to large firms. It locates a sphere of discretion for top echelons of private firms, being situated between the shareholders, on the one hand, and the workers, on the other. This senior management decision-making is strategic in orientation, to the extent that it concentrates upon goals and the selection of main action alternatives with a view towards the future (Brown *et al.*, 2004). How relevant is this concept to the public sector? Advocates of the New Public Management claim that strategic management fits well into public sector governance, although there are still sceptics who argue that public administration is the proper framework for the study of the execution and implementation of government policies (Fredrickson and Smith, 2003). Public administration underlines the rule-oriented nature of public sector decisions as well as the strong position of the politicians as the "owners" of public resources in deciding upon public sector ends and means. In contrast, strategic management in private firms presupposes that senior managers are at arm's length from the shareholders, as the top managers of private resources have enough autonomy to engage in decision-making about organisational ends and means in the future.

Reforms have pushed the public sector in the direction of strategic management (Ferlie *et al.*, 1996; Pollitt and Bouckaert, 2004), especially in countries where the New Public Management philosophy has been endorsed officially (Pollitt *et al.*, 2004). Agency autonomy has increased, as politicians often only concentrate upon goals, leaving the implementation of policy to so-called executive agencies. Policy objectives sometimes tend to be ambiguous and complex, leaving considerable space for alternative ways of executing policies. Finally, technology has developed, increasing the degrees of freedom in choosing among alternative means, for example, internet government. As politicians and agency chief executives sometimes work together in public sector governance, the question arises of how they can steer the organisation towards desired outcomes, or improved performance. What are some of the typical choices that senior management would face in public organisations? I suggest that the concept of strategic management may elucidate the situation.

Strategic management has no established definition. One may wish to remain sceptical as it smacks of fads and fashions. The question is, however, whether it is so similar to concepts such as strategic planning, comprehensive rationality and top-down management that it will be so critiqued that it falls apart (Mintzberg, 1993). Yet, strategic management should, rather, be linked with the theory of the new public organisation on the basis of the theory of contracting under asymmetric information – economic organisation theory that stresses incentives in contracting (Ricketts, 2003).

Strategy against tactics

It holds true that even though the concept of strategy is vague it is still highly useful for the analysis of decision-making processes, for instance, in military affairs, private firm management and in game theory in general (Dutta, 2000). With respect to the public sector, where agencies vary greatly in size from the minuscule to the gigantic, the public choice literature analyses several organisational strategies, including bureaux expansion, bureaux reshaping, bureaux autonomy and bureaux turf. Their analytical focus is the implications of the bureaucrat's egoism, which, sometimes, drives bureaux towards inefficient levels of output and the capture of slack, which, sometimes, shapes their activities towards prestigious tasks (Dunleavy, 1991). In public administration, there can be found a strong emphasis upon the collective, yet self-centred interests of an almost immortal or impenetrable agency, inevitably generating resistance to change and reinforcing established procedures (Kaufman, 1989).

The policy network approach, on the other hand, underlines the interdependency of agencies upon private partners in order to get the job done (Kickert *et al.*, 1997). The New Public Management suggested a strong remedy against both agency autonomy and agency inefficiency, namely, outsourcing the provision of services, or the contracting out of public services provision. Osborne and Hutchinson's (2004) version of reinventing government entails undoing the classical institutions of bureaucracy, and putting the provision of almost all services upon a system of short-term contracts. Today, there is a realisation of the limits of contracting out in the post-New Public Management era, as agencies attempt to focus upon their core activities, underlining the importance of achievement of social objectives over productivity (Brown and Osborne, 2005).

Strategic management in a post-New Public Management assessment of public service delivery would focus upon the achievement of social objectives of provision, taking them as the guiding indicators in the design of public organisations and their conduct of continuous operations. What matters first and foremost is the effectiveness of the agency in meeting its social obligations. The constant public sector reforms have, in many places, led to a hollowing out of the state (Peters and Savoie, 2000). The provision of public services has strong distributional consequences, which implies that state contraction leads to increased inequality or, even, more poverty. The occurrence of garbage can decision processes does not, however, undo the relevance of a normative framework focussing upon strategic management, as "is" does not entail "ought".

At the same time, public sector reforms have increased the awareness of the importance of strategic choices about how best to provide public services. Markets may provide, or help provide, services designated as "public" or "essential" and there are several ways to contrive market provision through the employment of various tendering and bidding schemes.

The theory of strategic management should be seen as a normative approach to public service delivery with no claim to being able to describe ongoing practices. Whether, and to what extent, this occurs is an interesting question but strategic management is more about what is feasible in terms of public sector reform. It asks: given the demand for efficiency, how is it best to design public organisations that are more prone to engage in strategic management, despite all the factors that lead to myopia, organisational slack and organisational autonomy?

The concept of strategic management, when employed for the analysis of decision-making, is complex and perhaps not a very precise one. It engulfs a variety of different kinds of decision-making: the lowest level of strategy is operational strategy, which deals with day-to-day operational activities, such as scheduling criteria. Business strategy is the aggregation of operational strategies of a single private firm or of strategic business units – semi-autonomous units within an organisation – that are responsible for their own budgeting, new product decisions, hiring decisions and commodity pricing decisions. In a diversified private firm, business strategy refers to the way in which it competes in its chosen market segments. Corporate strategy is the overarching strategy of the diversified private firm, answering questions such as: in which businesses should we compete? How does being in one business add to the competitive advantage of the corporation as a whole? The concept of dynamic strategy aims to portray firm strategy, both business and corporate, embracing ongoing strategic change and the seamless integration of strategy formulation and implementation. But these conceptions of strategy do not sit well in the public sector context, except perhaps, for the incorporated public enterprise. What is needed is a conception of strategic management that applies to the provision of core services by the public sector.

The specificity of public services and the limits of an algorithm for public services

A public service is not like a business area with a multi-purpose private firm operating in the marketplace:

- it is an activity undertaken by a political body, often governed through democratic political processes;
- its provision is regulated in public law, meaning that the public employees or bureaucrats providing these services have to act within the framework of rule of law (Lane, 1996);
- it is partly or wholly financed by taxes.

Strategic management has to accept these restrictions. What would strategic management signify? It belongs to the rational theory of organisation and it shares with other rationalistic approaches the weakness that it does not describe organisational reality accurately. It is easy to point out that in the public sector strategic management is political, which may raise much resistance and may end in organised chaos. But let us here focus upon the potentiality of strategic management; what its promise would be in a period of public sector reform.

Of course, strategic management would be constrained in the public sector. The politicians constitute the principal and the managers are merely their agents. The legal framework of the public sector would also narrow down choice options in order that rule of law may be accommodated. A most serious constraint is the lack of any viable or verifiable indicator of the value of public services that are not traded in the marketplace sector. While public services paid for wholly or partly by taxes do generate value, it is not easily measured. The problem is that strategic management seeks to maximise value, given choice constraints, but what if the measurement of value is not forthcoming automatically or unambiguously? The public manager must, thus, start the process of strategic management using a proxy measure of value, like, for instance, policy objectives and their corresponding outcome indicators. There are also other, more troublesome considerations to take into account when calculating a strategy for the provision of public services. These derive from the key insights into the way public administration works in reality and result from either self-interest seeking tactics (myopia) or confusion (ambiguity) on the part of participants, and they are very difficult to operationalise.

Objectives and the relevance of outcome indicators

Politics and politicians set more restrictions upon public organisations than do ownership boards on private firms. In public organisations, goals tend to be ambiguous and complex, meaning that the government would be more hesitant to delegate much decision-making on objectives to agency managers. Since public sector activities tend to be regulated by means of public law, the room for change is more confined. Yet, at the same time, agencies are not merely orientated towards the technical aspects in fulfilling goals handed down by politicians. Agencies participate in the discussion upon the selection of objectives, both by evaluating existing goals and suggesting new future goals. This stands in contrast to the private sector, where private owners, given that the goal of profitability is fulfilled, would not interfere in the conduct of a firm's strategies, although they would want to approve of major changes. This is not to deny that much of strategic management at the agency level consists of how best to get things done.

Strategic management is operational, meaning that it targets the structure of the main public service activities and determines how they are to be carried out. Whereas it used to be the case that there was one mode of production of public services – tax-financed bureaucracy – it is now the case that the choice among alternative forms of provision calls for deliberate strategic thinking. Strategic managers in the public sector face the problem of maximising or satisfying a set of goals, some derived from within the agency, while others are externally produced. Failure to achieve those goals will elicit criticism, albeit at the risk of being fired.

This is a fundamentally outcome-focussed perspective on public management. It is only viable if outcomes can somehow be measured and compared, and their meaning verified, in a non-costly manner. The development of evaluation methodology in the social sciences now allows for the employment of a variety of outcome measures. Such outcome criteria may target:

- number of services produced
- quality of services
- satisfaction with services
- quantity and distribution of services
- unit costs.

Strategic managers would face specific objectives for each of these outcomes, which would state the direction of change that managers need to embark on in order to achieve these objectives and, therefore, improve service outcomes.

It is, thus, the stated outcome indicators and their interpretation that should guide strategic management in the public sector. Most core public services are provided without charge and are funded through taxation, which means that strategic managers need some kind of information about what value they produce for end users. This means that the designated outcome measures become a proxy for the utility derived by public service end users and stakeholders. Outcome measures offer both benchmarks for the monitoring of activities and suggestions as to where improvements could be made. The agencies may wish to turn to professional policy analysts or evaluation specialists in order to have this outcome information. Without it strategic management would fumble in the dark, choosing alternative modes of organisation without key outcome reference points.

Team production: the relevance of stability and employee satisfaction

To achieve public service provision objectives, the strategic manager uses an allocation of resources, which used to be measured in terms of physical and labour resources but today is measured in terms of a financial allocation, allowing the managers more leeway as to the choice of production functions.

From the strategic point of view, the strategic public managers would face a few critical choices:

- the size of the team
- the composition of the team
- the allocation of tasks between internal production and outsourcing.

All three of these choices would be resolved, one way or the other, when the contracts are handed down and signed. At the end of the day, strategic management is about contracting. Performance and remuneration constitute the essential elements of contracting in the public sector, just as it is in the private sector. They will reflect the bargaining power of managers, on the one hand, and of employees, on the other.

In the classical model of public sector management the implementation of a master plan, calculating the optimal rates of performance given full knowledge of the effort levels of employees linked with alternative payment schemes, symmetric information and strategy-proof behaviour are assumed. Since all is, in principle, known or knowable, strategic management comes down to a question of computation, deriving a set of algorithms for performance-remuneration schemes that build upon sincerely held preferences and automatic enforcement of agreements. In reality, however, contracting always involves uncertainties, unknown and even unknowable risks, insincere preferences, tactical behaviour with guile, and asymmetric information (Hiller, 1997). Strategic management can only reduce these limitations upon rationality with redundancy, slack and duplication.

Size of the team

If there was a true algorithm available for the size of the crew to bring on board when sending out the airplane to deliver public services at some location, then strategic management would calculate the exact number that needs to be employed in-house or outsourced. Theoretically, given perfect information and no transaction costs, the optimal size of the workforce is that where the marginal product of labour is equal to the marginal cost of labour, with each unit of labour receiving remuneration corresponding to his or her marginal value product. However, in team production functions the exact value of these variables tend not to be known or to be unverifiable. The result is that teams tend to be larger than optimality and remuneration tends not to be set at the level of marginal productivities. Yet, the total value of the public services output must be greater than the total cost of its production, if the net value of that output is to remain positive, which means that the size of the team has to be cut back in order to achieve this outcome.

New Public Management launched an attempt to disclose the basic parameters of team production by aggressive outsourcing and contracting in. However, there is a definitive limit to the usefulness of such forms of contracting, as they lead to staggering transaction costs in relation to the making and enforcement of all the contracts and tournaments. Yet, in team production the optimal team size is seldom fully known, due to asymmetric information (Rasmusen, 2007).

Structure of the team or organisational design

Providing public services is a labour intensive process. Only recently has the massive employment of information technologies started to change the structure of organisations by empowering lower echelons to do more advanced work at the expense of middle-level supervisors. New insights from organisation theory, based upon the evolution of technology, suggest that the old model of bureaucratic organisation is no longer as relevant as it used to be (Kernaghan *et al.*, 2000). The relevance of strategic management thus needs to be evaluated in the context of the "new public organisation".

Organisational design is the design of an organisation's structure: functional, divisional and matrix. Functions or divisions belong to mechanistic organisations, which has been the traditional or classical design in many medium- and large-size organisations. It is rigid in form with often clearly-delineated jobs, a well-defined hierarchy with a formal chain of command for decision-making and control. In contrast, an organic structure is more flexible, and more adaptable to participative forms of management. Organic organisations that have a flat structure with only one or two levels of management – offering a decentralised approach to management – would stimulate greater employee involvement. A matrix organisation is one in which teams report to two or more managers. Matrix structures may include functional and divisional chains of command simultaneously in the same part of the organisation, commonly for one-of-a-kind projects. Boundary-less organisations are similar to flat organisations, with a strong emphasis on teams, where cross-functional teams dissolve horizontal barriers and enable the organisation to respond quickly to environmental changes and to spearhead innovation. The flat organisation calls for a learning organisation to facilitate team collaboration and the sharing of information; more able to adapt and respond to change than a hierarchical organisation. This design would empower employees to acquire and share knowledge and apply this information to decision-making.

The so-called "new public organisation" has a flat organisational structure instead of the hierarchical one, which would, somehow, have to be governed. If subordination in terms of a formal structure is not to be used, then perhaps only strategic management can direct teams towards the achievement of their objectives, to be evaluated in terms of either productivity or effectiveness, or both. No doubt, employee satisfaction has played a major role in the transition from a hierarchical organisational structure to a flat structure. Also, technology has made it possible to empower lower-level echelons. Thus, strategic management offers a tool for co-ordinating the activities of an agency that is less mechanistic and more boundary-less in form as well as learning (Ashkenas *et al.*, 1998).

Contracting and teams: monitoring versus transaction costs

Public service provision can be looked upon as a contracting problem with a huge set of contractual situations involving a variety of people: politicians, higher-level managers, middle-level managers and the street-level bureaucrats (for in-house provision), and contractors (for outsourced provision). Making use of the insights of economic organisation theory (Ricketts, 2003) strategic management, when used to determine the size and structure of teams, addresses the problem of mixing in-house production with outsourcing. In reality, this is a contractual question, which occurs in all forms of team production and involves three different types of contracts and their surveillance:

- long-term employment with monitoring versus short-term outsourcing with constant tendering;
- *ex ante* and *ex post* contract disparity;
- contract monitoring costs (in-house provision) versus switching costs (outsourced provision).

When people are employed in teams, then the contract tends to have a longer duration than used in conventional buy-and-sell situations – spot contracts (Milgrom and Roberts, 1992). Thus, there arises the question of the fulfilment of the contract *ex ante* as distinct from *ex post*. The two may not correspond. The disparity between them may be very large, raising all kinds of questions about verification and counter measures against contractual reneging. Monitoring used to constitute the classical tool for minimising this disparity, involving the taking of disciplinary measures before termination procedures are engaged. It comes, though, with a considerable cost in terms of running surveillance and taking disciplinary actions.

In the philosophy behind the New Public Management, switching contracts is a better method for minimising this disparity between *ex ante* and *ex post* contracts. Thus, the crucial issue now is whether monitoring costs are greater or smaller than switching costs. Advocates of the New Public

Management would be inclined to argue that switching costs are smaller than monitoring costs, given the likelihood of collusion among agents. There are simply too many tactics that can be used in monitoring, making it toothless.

Advocates of public administration would definitely argue that monitoring costs are smaller than switching costs, magnifying the costs of switching from one team to another. Two other considerations strengthen this proposition: stability in service provision and employee satisfaction.

Macro relevance of strategic management

Strategic management in the public sector is relevant not only to micro management, aiming at productivity and effectiveness in each policy area. Strategic management may also reflect on overarching matters such as how to marry ecology and policy. Environmental concerns may be introduced in all policy areas by means of the establishment of certain guiding principles, such as the elimination of externalities, the polluter pays principle and the choice of a mix between resilience (*ex post protection*) and precaution (*ex ante removal*) in relation to environmental risks.

If all public policies have environmental implications, then a so-called meta-policy could be devised that gives guidelines about how ecology concerns are to be worked into a variety of policies. Facing a century with growing energy shortages and increasing pollution, governments need to develop a conscious environmental strategy, taking both energy and ecology into account. Some governments have already established the central principle that any policy must have an environmental assessment tied to it. But this constitutes a new area of policy-making where problems are still looking for solutions and there is wide disagreement about which principles to employ.

Conclusion

The concept of strategic management is an essentially normative one, which may be critiqued for its lack of realist assumptions about how public organisations tend to operate in general. It belongs to the rational approaches to public sector decision-making, having to face up to the objections raised in public administration towards the possibility or probability of rational decision-making.

Yet, strategic management is not without merit when debating the direction of public sector reform. As a normative concept, it complements the traditional focus of public administration upon bureaucracy and the rule of law by emphasising the achievement of objectives through organisational design and the handling of contracts with the team responsible for public service provision. It fits well with the theory of the new flatter public organisation, using information technology massively – the boundary-less learning organisation. Such an organisation would need to defend its rationale through goals evaluation, done by strategic management with due respect for the constraints upon management that come from rule of law.

A concept of strategic management for public services would be relevant for the conduct of operations by public agencies or bureaux. However, it must take into account the specific features of the public sector as well as include the implications of rule of law. Given the heralded critique of the rational decision model, strategic management must take into account the lessons from public administration about bounded rationality and the garbage can process. Only outcome measures would constitute the starting-point in the derivation of public sector strategic management. Key decisions in team production relate to the employment of such outcome measures for both the monitoring of real activities as well as the reform of these activities. When the "new public organisation" replaces bureaucracy, then a flat organisation may actually need more of strategic management.

I link the concept of strategic management for the public services with the J.D. Thompson notion of all organisations operating under a *rationality assumption*. In 1967, he published *Organizations in Action: Social Science Bases of Administrative Theory*, one of the most influential books on organisations in the twentieth century. Organisations must explain to their environments how they use resources to produce goods and services. They may fail to attain rationality as efficiency, but the relevance of the question concerning the quid pro quo in organisations can never be denied, not even by scholars who claim that organisations are hypocritical, running along the garbage can path.

The concept of strategic management appears highly promising when interpreting what is happening in public service provision after the onslaught of the New Public Management. It underlines the relevance of designing public services delivery systems so that they can deliver outcomes by taking normal incentives in a team of people, insiders or outsiders, into proper consideration (Koch and Dixon, 2007).

Essential summary

1   In a public sector with several organisations working in networks to provide services, the problem of accountability and control may be solved by making use of strategic management.
2   Strategic management covers both micro aspects of policy such as the choice of institutional arrangements as well as decisions on staffing, but also macro aspects of policy, such as energy savings and environmental protection.

3   There is no guarantee that strategic management will be successful. It belongs to the rational approach to policy-making, and may fail due to faulty information or individual infighting among the strategic policy-makers.
4   Strategic management responds to the need for an institutional policy, outlining which mechanisms are to be employed in relation to different kinds of public services.
5   Strategic management may also be employed in constructing a policy towards the so-called public sphere, promoting social capital.
6   After the public sector reform period, public organisations have become flatter and boundary-less. They may employ alternative governance mechanisms. Strategic management is the reply to the question of how to compose teams for the provision of public services, how to motivate them and how to steer them. Strategic management must address the omnipresent principal–agent problems in setting up and governing public teams as bureaux, as policy networks or as tendering/bidding schemes.

Suggested readings

Ashkenas, R.N., D. Ulrich, T. Jick and S. Kerr (1998) *The Boundaryless Organization: Breaking the Chains of Organizational Structure*. San Francisco: Jossey-Bass.

Boyne, G.A., C. Farrell, J. Law, M. Powell and R. Walker (2007) *Evaluating Public Management Reforms: Principles and Practice*. Milton Keynes: Open University Press.

Brown, K. and S.P. Osborne (2005) *Managing Change and Innovation in Public Service Organizations*. London: Routledge.

Brown, S.E., R.C. Lamming, J.R. Bessant and P. Jones (2005) *Strategic Operations Management* (Second edition). Oxford: Elsevier Butterworth-Heinemann.

Dunleavy, P. (1991) *Democracy, Bureaucracy and Public Choice: Economic Explanations in Political Science*. London: Harvester Wheatsheaf.

Dutta, P.K. (2000) *Strategies and Games*. Cambridge, MA: The MIT Press.

Ferlie, E., L. Ashburner, L. Fitzgerald and A. Pettigrew (1996) *The New Public Management in Action*. Oxford: Oxford University Press.

Fredrickson, H.G. and K.B. Smith (2003) *The Public Administration Theory Primer*. Boulder, CO: Westview Press.

Hiller, B. (1997) *The Economics of Asymmetric Information*. Basingstoke: Palgrave Macmillan.

Johnson, G. and K. Scholes (eds) (2000) *Exploring Public Sector Strategy*. New York: Prentice Hall.

Joyce, P. (1999) *Strategic Management for the Public Services*. Milton Keynes: The Open University Press.

Kaufman, H. (1989) *Red Tape: Its Origins, Uses and Abuses*. Washington, DC: Brookings Institution.

Kernaghan, K., B. Marson and S. Borins (2000) *The New Public Organization*. Toronto: The Institute of Public Administration of Canada.

Kickert, W.J.M., E.H. Klijn and J.F.M. Koppenjan (eds) (1997) *Managing Complex Networks: Strategies for the Public Sector*. London: Sage.

Koch, R. and J. Dixon (eds) (2007) *Public Governance and Leadership: Political and Managerial Problems in Making Public Governance Changes the Driver for Re-constituting Leadership*. Wiesbaden: Gabler Edition Wissenschaft.

Lane, J.-E. (1996) *Constitutions and Political Theory*. Manchester: Manchester University Press.

McLaughlin, K., S.P. Osborne and E. Ferlie (eds) (2001) *The New Public Management: Current Trends and Future Prospects*. London: Routledge.

Milgrom, P. and J. Roberts (1992) *Economics, Management and Organization*. Englewood Cliffs: Prentice Hall.

Mintzberg, H. (1993) *The Rise and Fall of Strategic Planning: Reconceiving Roles for Planning, Plans, Planners*. New York: Simon and Schuster.

Mintzberg, H., B.A. Ahlstrand and J. Lamprel (1998) *Strategy Safari*. New York: Free Press.

Osborne, D. and P. Hutchinson (2004) *The Price of Government: Getting the Results We Need in an Age of Permanent Fiscal Crisis*. New York: Basic Books.

Peters, B.G. and D.J. Savoie (eds) (2000) *Governance in a Changing Environment*. Montreal: McGill-Queen's University Press.

Pollitt, C. and G. Bouckaert (2004) *Public Management Reform: A Comparative Analysis*. Oxford: Oxford University Press.

Pollitt, C., J. Caulfield, A. Smullen and C. Talbot (2004) *Agencies: How Governments Do Things Through Semi-autonomous Organizations*. Basingstoke: Palgrave Macmillan.

Rasmusen, E. (2007) *Games and Information*. Oxford: Blackwell.

Ricketts, M. (2003) *The Economics of Business Enterprise: An Introduction to Economic Organisation and the Theory of the Firm*. Cheltenham: Edward Elgar.

Stacey, R.D. (2007) *Strategic Management and Organisational Dynamics: The Challenge of Complexity*. Harlow: Prentice-Hall.

Index